IN NO TIME AT ALL

CARL HAMILTON

COURTESY USDA

IN NO TIME AT ALL

The Iowa State University Press / Ames, Iowa

CARL HAMILTON, vice-president of Information and Development, Iowa State University, was graduated from Iowa State University in 1936. Two and one-half years later, in 1938, he and Ruth Farnham Hamilton, newlyweds, traveled to Washington, D.C., where Carl was assigned to work with Claude Wickard, farmer from Indiana, who was administering the revolutionary new AAA. Carl accompanied Wickard when subsequently he was named Under-Secretary of Agriculture and then Secretary. During that heady decade, Carl and Ruth enjoyed the excitement of the Washington scene.

Carl left his government job in 1948 to fulfill his dream of running a country newspaper. In 1962, after fourteen satisfying years, he was asked to head the journalism department at Iowa State University; in 1965 he was appointed to his present position.

© 1974 The Iowa State University Press
Ames, Iowa 50010. All rights reserved

Composed and printed by
The Iowa State University Press

First edition, 1974.
   Second printing, 1974. Third printing, 1974.
   Fourth printing, 1975. Fifth printing, 1975. Sixth printing, 1975.

Library of Congress Cataloging in Publication Data

Hamilton, Carl, 1914–
   In no time at all.

   1. Farm life—Iowa.   2. Hamilton, Carl, 1914–
I. Title.
S521.5.I8H35   917.77′03′3 [B]   74–12346
ISBN 0-8138-0825-1

CONTENTS

V

VI

AN EXPLANATION

I STAND BETWEEN generations so to speak. My growing up experiences were during the twenties and thirties. Those, combined with the excellent memories of my sharp-minded, 89-year-old Mother, make it possible to look readily back to those fabled horse and buggy days.

On the other side of the equation, my wife and I have children who have jetted around the world and readily accept "space" in the context of other planets.

It is a cliché to emphasize the speed of change. And perhaps who cares but those who are living through it? But it appears (and that is all that can be claimed until historians look back from some distant vantage point) that we have gone through a phenomenon insofar as the rapidity of change is concerned. As the

saying goes, the horizons have disappeared and time has collapsed.

And collapsed so abruptly. We were moving along at a brisk clip before World War II. Then, all of a sudden, the dam burst and a whole way of life—particularly in rural areas—was erased in a twinkling.

Have we lost something in these changes? Or are the changes interesting only to those who have lived through them and a great bore to others who have come more recently upon the scene and are preoccupied with their own "life styles," as the saying goes these days? I pass no judgment. But if this effort does nothing else it may help succeeding generations, to whatever degree they want to be helped, to better understand the attitudes and motivations of the two generations of which I speak here.

Two final thoughts. You will run into references to The Four Families. They are included not because the names of Farnham, Walton, Heaton, and Hamilton are in any way more significant than the names of your own grandparents. They are included simply to give this effort a point of beginning—or background.

And finally (ah, this disclaimer will enrage the publisher!) this is not a "significant" book! Far from it. Interesting maybe. Amusing possibly. But in no way important. You see it all started out in an original so-called "family edition," no more than a series of essays for the benefit of Hamilton children. As I found my children remarkably interested in some of my mother's commentaries of another time, it occurred to me that recording some of these observations might be worthwhile. It was as innocent an effort as that. But one thing led to another and finally to this point. There is no plot. No message. No hidden meaning. It is for browsing. Or ignoring. Proceed accordingly. You have been warned.

Oh yes, royalties, if any, go to the Iowa State University Alumni Achievement Fund. Even if you don't care for the book, your purchase helps a worthy cause! Buy several.

CARL HAMILTON

Ames, Iowa
1974

To Those Who Helped

THE PERSON most responsible for this effort is my Mother. If she had not started telling her grandchildren of the olden days these essays never would have been undertaken. She criticized many of them, frequently observing they were written "from a man's viewpoint"—too much about threshing, not enough about preparing the dinner!

My sister Alice Walters helped a great deal, as did my wife Ruth.

Assistance in rounding up pictures came from Isabel Matterson, Iowa State University Library; Mary Cowell, Office of Information, USDA, Washington, D.C.; Don Muhm, farm editor, *Des Moines Register;* Al Bull, editor, *Wallaces Farmer,* Des Moines; and James Goodwin, Iowa Highway Commission, Ames.

To artist Ray Scott goes credit for the cover design and most credit of all goes to Kay Boyington who took rough copy to her kitchen table and turned out the finished manuscript. She was a combination typist, copy editor, and counselor.

The oversights and the errors? They are all mine.

CH

THE FOUR FAMILIES

THE NAMES Walton, Farnham, Heaton, and Hamilton speak to their points of origin. That Anglo-Saxon ring and some scattered records indicate that most of those families were here in time to help Mr. Washington in his affair with the British and did, in fact.

But we will skip over the better part of a century and take up our story when those names began to show up among the early settlers and first permanent residents in west central Iowa and in eastern Nebraska.

WALTON: By the late 1860s a railroad was pushing north out of Omaha. Twenty-five miles to the north another railroad was pushing west across the muddy Missouri. At the junction a town was born: Blair, Nebraska.

A young man there when all that was taking place was Wellington C. Walton. Born in Michigan in 1844, he presumably "read law" in that state, but maybe after he got to Nebraska. He was 25 or 26. Why did he come to Blair? Why was the West settled?

For the better part of the next half century he was to be an important person in that frontier area—district judge, state senator, prominent lawyer, mayor.

The Lantry brothers came to Nebraska to homestead. Their sister joined them. She married W. C. Walton and their daughter was Gertrude Farnham, mother of Ruth Farnham Hamilton.

FARNHAM: In 1886 Pittsfield, Massachusetts, must have been a community of some consequence and creature comforts. But still 49-year-old William Farnham sold his woolen mill, packed up his wife and son and moved halfway across the new nation. They took up homesteading 9 miles north of Blair.

Why would they leave an established community and take

up the harsh life of a homesteader on this not very prepossessing piece of real estate? They stuck to the land until 1894 when they moved to Blair where William, the woolen maker and homesteader, became, unaccountably, a watchmaker and jeweler.

The son, Charles, became a druggist and, late in life, married the only daughter of Judge Walton. Their daughter, and only child, was Ruth.

HAMILTON: Like William Farnham, Robert A. Hamilton was an established businessman in Strawn, Illinois, when, in 1890—at age 40 and with a large and growing family—he traded his store for a half section of land 10 miles northeast of Glidden, Iowa, on the very east edge of Carroll County. The trip to town and back was an all-day trek with team and wagon.

One of the Hamilton boys, Burton, was to complete his education in the nearby country school, court "the Heaton girl" with horse and buggy, and together they would begin their lifetime of farming on "the old Hamilton place."

Subsequently they moved to Wisconsin, then back to Clay County, Iowa, and then back to a series of rented farms near Glidden.

Their children, Carl and Alice, 4-H work and all that, were to end up at the people's college in Ames. Here Carl was to meet Ruth Farnham whose parents had encouraged her to attend an institution that would provide an education of value in the marketplace. The time: Depression.

HEATON: Alfred J. Heaton had been a butter maker in upper New York State. He came first to Illinois and by 1881 he had moved on west to Glidden where he went into the creamery business. The creamery burned and he moved on to a poor river-bottom farm northeast of Glidden—not far from where the Hamiltons would be settling very shortly.

Alfred and his wife had three children, only one of whom—Imogene—survived. She was "that Heaton girl," who would marry Burton Hamilton and become the mother of Carl and Alice.

Thus these four families had all "come west" and settled in western Iowa or on the Missouri River between the late 1860s and 1890. They came as permanent residents, planning to stay put. They were the "second wave" so to speak.

XII

The "first wave"—barely a ripple—were the pioneers, the true early settlers. These families lived by their wits, settling along streams, hunting, fishing, gardening, growing a little corn. Alfred Heaton's wife came from one of those truly early settler families.

Here's a snippet from the experiences of that family:

The first three white families to arrive in Carroll County settled along the Raccoon River northeast of Glidden. There they found timber for fuel and building and also artesian wells; they had good water the year around. Otherwise, they were without resources, isolated, and in not very hospitable surroundings. A year after their arrival, and after having been visited by sometimes demanding bands of Indians, they heard about the Spirit Lake Massacre.

One of those first three families was named Ochampaugh. A daughter, Nancy, would be Imogene Heaton's aunt and early-day stories were to come down through "Aunt Nancy McCoy."

Aunt Nancy was 15 and Uncle James 21 when they married. She was proud of her log cabin because it had a window and a door. Uncle James was a carpenter and had bought glass for the window when he went to Des Moines for cornmeal and to get their mail. Trip: 90 miles! Uncle James was also the casket maker in the community. Aunt Nancy used her wedding dress as lining material for baby coffins.

A check of old cemeteries tells a sad story. In the Benan Cemetery (where Imogene's ancestors are buried), markers show the deaths of five children in the same family in one month in the summer of 1883 . Often a grave is marked with the mother's name, "_____, wife of _____, and babe."

Aunt Nancy reared six boys in the log cabin. Among other things she once pieced a quilt. It had to be done in the summertime as smoke from the fireplace would stain it if done during the winter. Indians came by and took a fancy to her handiwork. They demanded it. She refused. After all it had been a lot of work and her family needed it!

Late one winter Uncle James went to Des Moines for mail and supplies. The thaws came and the streams flooded. He was stranded many days. The family ran out of food and Aunt Nancy ground corn for the family in the coffee mill!

Earlier we spoke of all that has happened during these last few decades. A lot happened between 1850 and 1890, too!

*   *   *

XIII

This, then, is the tiniest little thumbnail sketch of the Four Families and their appearance here on the midwestern scene, so recently the undisputed domain of the Indians and the buffalo. How sad that the records of their trials and hardships and disappointments—and their accomplishments, too—are so few.

Of those Four Families, only Imogene Heaton Hamilton, courted with horse and buggy, is still with us in 1974.

Following are Carl and Ruth Farnham Hamilton, four children and five grandchildren.

Change the names and this might be the story of your family!

XIV

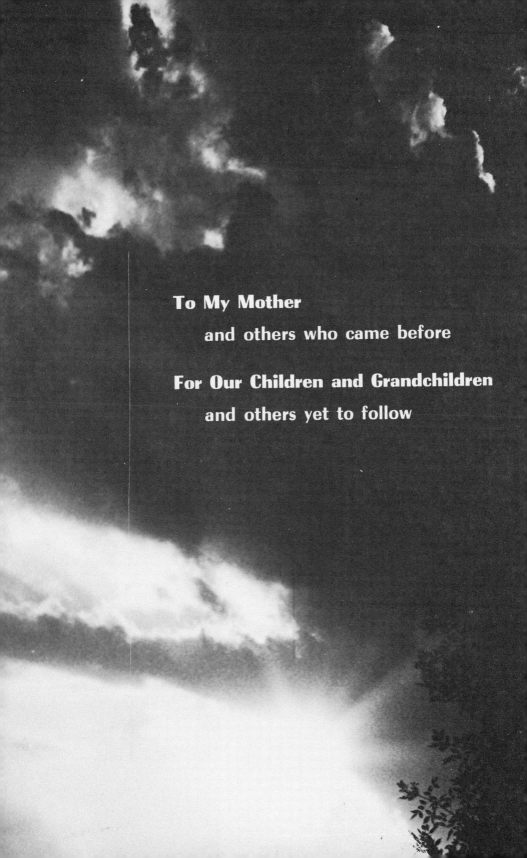

To My Mother
and others who came before

For Our Children and Grandchildren
and others yet to follow

PART ONE   THE DAY

BEGAN AT 5 A.M.

Morning: A Time That Poets Missed

SPRING MORNINGS on our farm began at 5 A.M. Probably they were not much different fifty years ago than today except they began earlier. In the olden days the pace of farm life was always steady and hard; the tempo quickened even more when the hired man came to work on March 1.

It was a few weeks before oats seeding but much work was to be done: manure to be hauled, machinery to be repaired, harness to be fixed, oats to be fanned. It was the calving, lambing, and farrowing seasons with lots of chores. After all, the hired man was there and he was making no money for the establishment by lying in bed. So it was getting up at 5 o'clock in the morning from March until the corn was picked—by Thanksgiving time, if all went well.

Of course the kind of horsepower we had was a major reason for early rising. If it was early in the spring and the horses were in the barn, it had to be cleaned out, the horses fed, curried, and harnessed. On summer nights they would be out in the pasture, but they had to be brought to the barns and put through the same process. Activity hummed between 5 A.M. and when the teams would start for the field at 7.

Ah, but summer mornings at 5 o'clock were in great contrast to the dirt and dust and drudgery that marked so much of the rest of farm life about which so much has been written by so many who have never been there. It was cool. The sun was perhaps an hour away. The countryside was quiet; so quiet. No cars. No

3

tractors. The chickens were coming slowly out of the hen house, stretching and fanning slowly out across the barnyard. The milk cows were at some spot out in the pasture where they had spent the night. Smoke began to rise slowly out of the kitchen chimney as Mother lit the cobs. Down the road another wisp of smoke appeared as the same drama was being reenacted at the neighbor's. A pheasant would speak up from a fence row retreat.

Dew would be heavy on the grass and the boy would slip into his rubber boots to head out to the pasture. Not until he was close enough to give the cows a nudge with his boot would they rise slowly, stretch, and, as though reluctant to start the day, amble toward the buildings. Shortly the boy, his dog, the cows, and the horses were moving slowly toward the barns. The day had begun. Still, the quietness of the countryside; the languid, unhurried way in which all living things had begun their day's activities; the softness of the sky just before sunup; the first birds —all seemed to be saying, "This is living; may this go on forever."

I hated to get up like any boy. But once up, I knew I was enjoying something special. I've experienced nothing quite like it since.

Mother used to share my sentiments, calling this "the nicest part of the day." It was. It was a slice out of rural America of the kind that Thomas Jefferson must have had in mind.

Three Moves Are as Bad as a Fire

THE HAMILTONS MOVED from the old Hamilton farm north of Ralston, northeast of Glidden, to St. Croix Falls, Wisconsin, in 1918. About three years later they moved back to a farm in Clay County, northwest Iowa, 12 miles west of Spencer. Two years later they moved back to the Glidden area—first to the "Brand place" south of Glidden, then to the "Black place" north of Ralston, and then back to the "Ingersoll place" a mile west of Glidden.

4

Three of those five moves were accomplished by rail. Everything we owned—furniture, clothes, livestock, machinery, tools, the cats, the dog, everything—was loaded on freight cars. Of course, first everything had to be hauled in lumber wagons, in some cases several miles, then loaded and packed in freight cars, along with enough feed for the livestock while it would be in transit. Even our auto was shipped by train.

Dad would then ride along, either in the caboose or in one of the cars, so that he could look after the livestock. When we left for Wisconsin we had neighbors and friends who helped load. But I have often wondered how Dad went about unloading those cars of machinery and livestock when he arrived in Wisconsin or at Moneta, a town of about seventy-five, where he knew not a soul.

In the case of Moneta, Dad had been there before Mother and Alice and I arrived early one morning on the Rock Island. He met us at the station with a horse and buggy. We started for what was to be home just as the school bus was coming down the road. It was horse drawn, of course, with side curtains and the kids were peering out at "the new family."

As the two rigs approached, one hind wheel on our buggy began to collapse. The spokes, rotten from age and lack of paint, gave way one at a time. We essentially had a flat wheel. It was bumping along, getting worse and worse, making a lot of noise and causing Old Pete to be more than ever "up on the bit."

So Dad followed the usual farmer remedy. He got a piece of barbed wire from the fence and tied that broken wheel so that the good side was held in the down position. That wheel functioned as a runner.

Under those sorry conditions the kids on that bus met "the new kids." I can still remember that morning. It was not an auspicious beginning.

But even on those moves within the same community, it was not a case of calling the moving van with packing quilts and boxes. In the first place, moving started in the fall. There might be snow on the ground on the traditional March 1 moving day and so everyone would begin picking items up and getting them inside or standing up along a building so they wouldn't be left behind. March always came in like a lion on those years in which we moved.

Along in January or February, if there were good relationships with the family vacating the farm to which you were moving, you started moving various items of equipment and machinery. It had to be carefully put to one side at the new place so as not to be in the way.

As the fatal day grew closer, packing was started in the house —really weeks ahead of time—and it grew increasingly hard to find things. The house grew more and more barren as curtains came down, rugs were rolled up, and the house began to have that hollow, empty ring.

Some neighbors pitched in to help on the final day. It was miserable: the men were never as careful as Mother thought they should be; everything was loaded in lumber wagons; some things got broken; there was no insurance; thus there was a loss of necessities or family keepsakes. All this only added to the trauma of the much-dreaded moving day.

Dad was always careful to see we had a better than average place to live but he couldn't select the new place because the rooms were the right size or the furniture would fit or we liked the decorating scheme. The new place was selected because of its farming opportunities and the "improvements"—meaning the barns, cribs, and sheds.

Farmers were and still are accused of "building the barn before the house." Some truth in that, too, because the "living" *is* in the barn and out in the fields.

Moving was always harder on Mother than anyone else. Frequently it was a case of moving into a house where the other family had "just moved out." It needed a thorough cleaning before moving in but there was no time. Rugs didn't fit; curtains didn't fit; cupboards didn't fit. The floors were bare pine boards with quarter-inch cracks and painted around the edges. The rugs seldom matched the unpainted areas.

There was no hot water until the cookstove was set up and going. Each room echoed with a hollow, unwelcome sound. The chill of March was throughout the house. If there was electricity, its evidence was found in a bare bulb casting its glare from a cord in the center of the ceiling.

As I look back on those times I think of Mother and Dad picking corn by hand in those years when they couldn't afford to hire help. But ranking next to that scene in my mind is Mother's lot at moving time. Throughout her years, the date of March 1 was always the subject of some comment on her part for "those poor people who are having to move." The sight of a load of

6

*Moving day—unhappy time! Neighbors came and
necessities and keepsakes alike took their chances on
scratches, breakage, and loss.*

household goods or machinery going down the road brought stabs of memories which I am sure were some of her most unhappy ones.

The Years We Lived beside the Prairie

THE HAMILTON "STOPOVER" in Clay County, in northwest Iowa, was not a particularly happy time but for me it had certain advantages. I was just old enough (8–10) to ride a horse, carry a rifle, and spend a good deal of time with the Bruggman boys across the road. I was also just a shade too young to do any real farm work.

One of the fascinations of that place was that our farm adjoined a considerable tract of original prairie. It had been a little tougher to tile than the surrounding acres. We didn't realize, of course, that our playground—with horses, rifles, and kid games— was Iowa's vanishing heritage: chunks of unplowed Iowa land were not so uncommon as to be given much of a thought.

I don't recall who claimed that land. Someone made up "prairie" hay each year and the stacks added excitement—a new place to hide. In swales where it was too wet to mow, the grasses grew tall and coarse and attracted the redwing blackbirds and other birds which didn't mean anything to 10 year olds. Meadowlarks and other "ground types" abounded, along with ground squirrels which we hunted with our .22s. Trails led aimlessly off across the tract and at various places good-sized holes provided homes for some burrowing animals. We were convinced coyotes and foxes were to be found there—and they were not unknown— but for the most part the holes we explored were the work of a neighborhood dog.

Nevertheless, the unbroken sod furnished natural habitats for birds, civet cats, some real life-sized skunks, squirrels—and lots of other things in our imagination.

But as we raced our horses around the stacks and took potshots at anything which came within our view, we didn't have

8

enough wonderment to appreciate the wildflowers or the prairie grasses and to realize that in just a few years drainage would turn that area into rich black loess corn land—that surpluses would bring 10-cent corn and that federal programs would later identify those acres to be "set aside."

When Once-a-Week Bathing Was Sufficient

AFTER LEAVING the old Hamilton place in 1918–1919 all our houses had electricity. That was pretty remarkable, considering that only 10 percent of America's rural homes had electricity until REA came into the picture in the early thirties. But the kilowatts were strictly for light. So we had plenty of opportunity to get acquainted with unmodern means of bath-taking. In Clay County we had a bathtub in the pantry where the bath water ran out a drain in the side of the house. It was filled, a pail at a time, from the kitchen range. In winter the pantry was a little frosty so we all swabbed off in the washtub in front of the range.

The idea of bathing more than once a week never occurred to us except in summer when a tub could be filled with water almost anyplace.

Windsor Folding Bath Tub

A comfort for outlying homes, not provided with plumbing facilities. Easy to operate, compact, neat and serviceable. Mounted on ball bearing casters. Occupies space about 30 inches square, when folded. Tub is 5 feet long, 30 inches wide. Heavy sheet steel. White enamel paint finish. Hardwood rim. Frame and platform durably built of steel. Nickeloid heater with heavy galvanized steel lining. Water is heated by copper coils. State whether wanted for gas, kerosene or gasoline. Furnished with 4 feet of hose and hose connection for draining. Shipping weight, 170 pounds.
281 C 6424...............**$36.95**
Shipped from Detroit

One of the unique items which came along with the move to the "Black place," north of Ralston, was a bathtub of a kind I have never seen elsewhere. It was a little like a Murphy or fold-up bed. It was a tub shaped much like a conventional tub but mounted on a frame on wheels. When in use it would be rolled

9

out in the kitchen or wherever one chose to expose himself to soap, water, and general public gaze. It had a hose attached to the outlet and that could carry the bath water out the door or into some drain.

But once the event was finished, the tub could be upended and folded into its rack, on casters, so that it could be wheeled into the pantry or spare room where it was kept.

A real step forward. One could bathe without sitting cross-legged in a round washtub! What could we look for next!

Of course, with all these processes, no matter what the "medium," it took a little close planning at those times of the year when the family and the hired man had to coordinate their time in the tub. On the "Black place" the family slept upstairs in two rooms, the entrance to the second being through the first. The hired man slept downstairs. So, once the family was scrubbed, we all retired and the hired man had the "bathroom" to himself—if he wanted to bathe!

Saturday Night and Another Week Done

GOING TO TOWN on Saturday night during the summer was a ritual. It was a family affair and for the hired men too, although they went their separate ways. There was an attempt (mild on Dad's part) to push along a little faster late Saturday afternoon or with the chores. Supper was hurried. There was a lineup for the bathtub. Someone got the 12-dozen case of eggs and carried it out to the car. Also a can of very sour cream, although that was a pretty small thing with us. Milking was not Dad's thing.

Heat had gone out of the day. In shirt-sleeves and cotton dresses, the family putted off to town, the breezes pleasant in an open car. You checked on the height of the neighbor's corn, how he was getting along cultivating, the size of his spring pigs.

You wouldn't believe it, but the biggest problem was park-

Saturday night in town was the week's major social event.
Trading eggs and cream for flour, yeast, sugar, and other
such necessities was the excuse for the trip.

ing. Not that room to park in wasn't plentiful in a town of 800.
Or that the distance to walk with the eggs and the groceries was
too great. The point was to get a spot on Main Street, preferably
near the most popular grocery store or near "the corner."

Dad couldn't care less about this matter. Nor I. But to
Mother and Alice it was important. Because as soon as the eggs
were candled and the trading done, "the women" were uncom-
fortable "just standing around" out on the street as the men
would do. So they hoped the car was parked somewhere close to
the action, where they could perhaps find a neighbor or a relative
to join them, visit, and "just watch the people." It was fun. You
knew virtually everyone you saw as they "visited" up and down

the sidewalk, discussing the weather, the crops, family illnesses, and just plain gossip. The younger kids, reunited for a few hours, ran up-and-down the street and through the alleys. The slightly older ones, old enough to drive, would concentrate on some boy whose parents were fortunate enough to have a new car. If he was lucky enough to "borrow it" for a brief period they would tool out to the freshly paved Lincoln Highway and marvel when the car rolled up to 60 miles an hour. Then they would hurry back to Main Street—before they were missed, they hoped.

Dad and his counterparts would gather in front of the hardware or harness shop, lean against the buildings, or squat on a curb or bench and talk horses, hired men, prices, and the weather.

The barber shops on Saturday night would be jammed and barbers would be clipping away until 11 o'clock or later—and giving more than an occasional shave. Somebody, more than likely a hired man, was getting "fixed up for Sunday." All the customers were "two-toned." Protected by straw hats, their foreheads were white as bakers' bread, but their face, neck, ears, and forearms were tanned, ruddy, and rugged. I didn't go to the barber shop. Dad cut my hair until I went away to college. This was a Hamilton habit that hung on; I followed the same practice with my sons and for an equally long time!

When we got to town, Dad would reach in his pocket and give me some change. No set amount and never as much as a half dollar; more nearly a quarter. Sometime during the evening I and the four or five boys I would always run into would get a dish of ice cream at Tom Roberts's soda fountain. When we got home I would put the change on the kitchen table. That was before the days of allowances.

Along about 10 o'clock the crowd would begin to thin out. The groceries and the empty egg case would be in the back seat. The family would assemble at the car and drive home through the cool of the night. The week was done.

The Catalog: A Medium of Change and Use

TELEVISION has put strange stresses on our society. It is damned for stimulating our expectations which we then find beyond our ability to satisfy. This creates tensions, we are told; that is bad.

Well, at an earlier time and on a less extensive scale, those same charges should have been leveled at another uniquely American institution: the mail-order catalog.

We are led to believe too that our moral fiber is being eroded at present by credit cards, installment buying, and easy credit! Study the old catalogs. Throughout the whole book were $5 down and $5 a month temptations.

When the average farm home, uncluttered by radio or television, had only a weekly and possibly a daily newspaper and some magazines, the arrival of a Montgomery Ward or Sears and Roebuck catalog was a major event.

It was carefully studied by parents as they compared prices in their never-ending struggle to match resources with necessities. "Making out the order" was a project that might go on for some weeks and would include everything from long underwear to farm tools. Clearly desires must have been stimulated beyond means by the long hours of studying the vast array of merchandise with prices which ranged from Good to Better to Best.

The arrival of the catalog was even more of an event for the kids. Hours and hours of long winter evenings and rainy Sunday afternoons were spent thumbing through that catalog—a page at a time! Pictured and described in mouth-watering detail were goodies of another world: guns and traps . . . jackknives in wondrous variety . . . saddles and fancy bridles . . . leather jackets like some of the town kids wore . . . fancy gloves . . . high-laced boots . . . musical instruments . . . toy steam engines . . . erector sets . . . page after page after page!

I knew them all by heart. I was going to be a hero playing one of those shiny trumpets. My .22 was my pride and joy but, oh boy, all those high-powered rifles and pistols and shotguns. And high-laced boots. Town boys had them and I would wear out those pages which described their comforts and advantages: "all genuine cowhide, warm, dry, no need for overshoes, etc." Eventually Mother did give in and I got a pair.

"The wish book" was an important document in the house.

But what an ignominious end it had. One so in keeping with the times: waste nothing! Where did that valued, much-treasured book end up? In the privy! There, of course, it served a double purpose. It served as "tissue"—although hardly of the scented, soft-textured brands of milady's toilette. Also it provided one last chance to review the well-studied pages. And, providing the weather was right, meaning it wasn't so cold as to bring chilblains to unaccustomed places or so warm as to encourage flies, the catalog added interest to that interlude in the day's activities. Of course, it did have limitations even for that final purpose. Even under the most extreme circumstances, when nothing was being wasted, the slick paper sections did leave something to be desired as "tissue." There came a time when the remains—the high fashion section—was consigned en masse to the lower regions! Kerplop!

He Gave No Number; He Just Demanded

THE FIDELITY of the average country telephone, even up until World War II and after, was just about one step removed from Alexander Graham Bell's first effort.

But that thin wire, sometimes hanging on fence posts and often needing repair, did hold a community together. A "line call" would alert everyone to a local problem—taking the place of the 7 A.M. school closing announcements over today's radio station.

Dad was a man of direct action when it came to wanting to get someone on the phone. If it was someone on our line we all knew the ring—two longs and a short, for example—and you did just that, assuming that there was no one on the line.

But if it was a number through Central, Dad didn't waste any time looking up anybody's number. He would give Central a good sharp ring and when she inquired "Number, please?" he would rather bluntly demand, "Get me Doc Wagner!" And she

14

would. Doc Wagner was the local veterinarian. None of the rest of the family had quite the audacity to handle Central like Dad did. But he got away with it. And just as well. She knew all the numbers and rings anyway.

Oh yes, you always gave the phone a wide berth during thunderstorms; lightning would come in and give you a solid little jolt!

You Mean They Didn't Want REA?

RURAL DELIVERIES of mail were being made in some parts of the nation before the turn of the century. But not until about World War I did it become general. Mother recalls Granddad Heaton "worked to get a route started" out of Scranton before such service became general. The Heatons were readers.

As at present, those who had fought in our wars were given the opportunity to carry our mail. Mother recalls the first rural mail carriers as "poor old veterans" driving those long, lonesome miles with horse and buggy through summer's rains and winter's blizzards.

Telephone service came by fits and starts, often with locally organized "farm mutuals." "We felt pretty isolated," Mother recalls, "until there was phone service." When her sister was severely burned it was necessary to drive 2 miles with team and buggy to get to a neighbor's home with a phone.

The fidelity of the early phone service was unbelievable by present-day standards. Of course, the dry-cell batteries may have been weak. But even under the very best of circumstances, you often shouted your message and each conversation was interrupted many times by "Speak up, I can't hear you." Afterward, we wondered—had there been complete understanding on either end of the line?

That doesn't mean there wasn't "visiting" on country lines; there was. People were lonesome and it was a "contact with the outside world." But it took effort.

Small competing phone companies came into the picture very early and not infrequently a small town would be served by two different systems. If you were on one you could talk only to the people on that system. Generally there were no interconnections.

Only about one farm in ten had electricity when the New Deal came into business in 1932. It came slowly, but with government encouragement and low-interest loans, the Rural Electrification Administration, REA as it was known, spread across the nation and had lights in most rural homes fairly soon after World War II.

Phone service, however, still remained next to nonexistent— at best very bad—in great sections of rural America. So REA, in which I had worked, was authorized to start doing the same thing for rural communications it had done for rural power. Just as I was resigning from REA in Washington a rural telephone loan was being made to a group of farmers in the Iowa Falls community where I was to take up my newspapering responsibilities. I gave this effort full support, writing editorials about how it was easier for me to call Washington than neighboring Owasa, which indeed it was. My advocacy was welcomed with something less than total enthusiasm by officials of the Bell system. Even vice-presidents from Des Moines drove up to entertain this brash young editor who was infecting the countryside with these socialistically tainted ideas from Washington. Just give them time, they said, and they would come in and assure the kind of service that rural areas so much desired. But be patient, they urged. Right now they didn't have either the money or the equipment to do what was required. They especially emphasized the need for capital.

Well, when that group of farmers actually began to firm up plans for getting under way with their government loan, Ma Bell suddenly found both funds and equipment. They took over the local mutual companies and shortly had trucks all over the place. In no time at all we had good rural service!

In many respects, the rural electrification story is even more unbelievable. It was tough going to push those lines out across the countryside, to get people to "sign up." A farmer signing up had to put $5 on the line. It was a co-op effort and some of his more aggressive neighbors were soliciting memberships, house-to-house. Everyone had to sign up to make the loan "feasible."

16

COURTESY *Farm Town: A Memoir of the 1930's*

Farmers, working with the new thing called REA,
stretched lines out across rural America, brought lights
to their homes, and wrought the single greatest change
ever to occur in farm life.

Many resisted, believing it was all some kind of hoax; they just couldn't believe that anything would bring lights right into their homes. The commercial power companies had been telling farmers for years that it wasn't economically feasible to take power lines out across rural areas, particularly for such small loads.

The first loans, with a lot of blue sky thrown in, were projected on the basis that farmers might use as many as 75 kilowatts

17

a month! Quicker than anyone could believe it, many farmers were using 1,000 a month. It was obviously a rich market and the struggle between co-ops and the investor-owned utilities took on classic proportions in many areas.

Looking back now, almost four decades, and recalling how difficult it was to sell the idea of electricity in rural areas, tells more about the rate and depth of change in rural America than almost anything else that can be recalled or told. Rural electrification did more to change rural America than any other single thing.

An "Agent" Came to Call

THE IDEA of a county agent—someone driving into your yard and offering some new information without charge—that was something new! This startling concept, coming onto the scene about World War I, had implications for the development of this country that went far beyond the comprehension of those who passed the law back in Washington.

The young ag college graduate would begin a kind of Johnny Appleseed operation—spreading the word about clean ground for raising hogs, corn-corn-oats and clover rotations, and something called "balanced rations." The Home Demonstration Agent (HDA) was similarly busy with the homemakers.

Not every new idea was to catch fire (like the great idea of making and selling capons rather than those leggy roosters).

Neutralizing the sex of male calves and pigs was a routine rainy-day farm operation. Dad's jackknife (he felt as naked as without pants when he didn't have his favorite four-bladed knife in his pocket) had a special blade for surgical processes. The glands of pigs and calves being located in obviously accessible places, this operation was no big deal. Just a two-man or a man-and-a-boy job. Do it on a rainy day when no dust would get in the opening and recovery could be remarkably rapid.

Technology came to the farm by horse and buggy. Early
cow testers used rigs like this as they pulled into farmers'
yards to test the butterfat content of milk samples from
the dairy herd.

With roosters, well, that's something else again. The county
agent, however, suggested that caponizing young roosters really
was a home-talent kind of operation and that the resulting price
advantage of capons over roosters, with their added tenderness
and size, would make it a rewarding undertaking.

Well, unfortunately, there turned out to be more "undertaking" in it than he—or we—had anticipated! The rooster was
stretched out on a board, the feathers were peeled off of a part of
his midsection, a small slit was made through the skin and flesh,
and you peered into the darkness of his inner workings—hopefully
within sight of his maleness. Maleness in this instance was about
the size of a pea and was to be removed with a pair of forceps sharp
enough for the necessary detachment.

In this fairly delicate little exercise, vision was totally re-
stricted once the forceps were in the opening. So by feel you
snipped. But if you mis-snipped, your bird didn't turn into a
capon; he turned into an immediate fryer! He quickly bled to
death. Well, you could only accommodate about so many fried

19

chickens at any one time—especially without refrigeration. Caponizing didn't catch on!

Of course, the counterpart of that is one of the most hilarious stories I have ever heard James (Jimmie) Hilton tell. As part of his preparation for later becoming—among other distinguished things—president of Iowa State University, he was county agent in Greene County, Iowa, in the early 1920s.

Jimmie was giving a hog butchering demonstration. The farmers all gathered around to see what this fresh young graduate from "the college" could teach them about this well-known practice.

First, said the bright young fellow, you put Mr. Pig over on his back—which he was able to do with the help of some in his audience. Then you deftly stick a knife in exactly the right spot on the exposed neck, give it just the right twist, cut the proper vein, let the doomed porker back on his feet and he quickly bleeds to death.

All went well throughout the early stages of the procedure. The knife was inserted and Jimmie gave it the proper twist. The pig was let back on his feet. Obviously not overly pleased with his roll-over-and-be-quiet part of the little drama he simply shook his head and ambled off across the yard—to the great and everlasting embarrassment of the new county agent. Jimmie's knife had not found the mark!

But the success stories of the county agents and the HDA's, now known as county extension directors and home economists, are all justified. When the county agent stopped in to visit there was time to stop and listen.

In the beginning they and their new information were not accepted without questioning. When we lived near Moneta a farmer known as "an Ames farmer" lived over on the other corner of the section. He had been to school "down at the college." He tried a lot of highfalutin' things; best just watch him, do it "the other way," and you would probably be better off.

But those doubters soon had another complaint. "The college" and its agents—by whatever name—couldn't get the information out fast enough. Farmers tried to get an early peek into the researcher's test tube, urging him to "go faster."

Of course, the real grabber for the county agent and his HDA

20

associate was something called 4-H. This became general in the early twenties. My sister, I, and all the neighboring kids were in 4-H. When the county agent dropped in to see your calf it was a pretty big deal. One of my calves was named after H. I. Axtell who was our county agent. The county agent was that important.

Much of the HDA's stress was on "making ends meet." This effort included sewing and home canning of everything including meat. Later, when some brash New Dealers came to a parting of the ways with extension, they pointed to extension's old-fashioned ways and declared that HDA's were teaching farm women how to make underclothes out of feed sacks and furniture out of orange crates when they should have been teaching the art of revolution: "Throw off your chains!" (That really meant vote Democratic and throw out the Farm Bureau!)

With that comment, let me turn to a political sidelight of the county agent story that will be of interest to some.

The new county agent, dropped down in the county seat without any mechanism to tell his story other than the weekly paper, found his effectiveness might be quickened if some supporting organizations were developed. So "farm bureaus" came into existence. Initially, these were politically innocent tools for helping spread the good word. But they did not so remain. In a long and complicated process those "farm bureaus" grew into state farm bureaus and finally into a powerful national farm bureau, the American Farm Bureau Federation. For some four decades the efforts of the land-grant colleges and the USDA were tied legally and philosophically as well to that powerful, politically active organization.

Obviously both efforts were concerned in one way or another with the welfare of farm people. But the conflict of interest was obvious and grew more so.

County agents, hired to be educators, found their salaries were enhanced if there were more farm bureau members. Thus they actively worked at selling memberships with one hand while with the other they attempted to fill the role of the wholly objective educator. That this incredible conflict was allowed to continue now seems beyond belief. Mother, until she retired from the farm, spoke of going to extension organized meetings as going to "take the farm bureau work."

21

Planking a Major Transcontinental Highway

"THE BOTTOM just dropped right out!"

That was the description of Iowa's roads and highways each spring until some 18-foot concrete slabs began to reach across the state in the 1920s.

Before gravel, Iowa's country roads, just plain dirt, were a quagmire in the spring and after each rain. But it didn't make a lot of difference. Most vehicles were horse drawn and cars just stayed home until the sun did its work.

But by the twenties, cars and light trucks were demanding year-round service—regardless of weather—particularly on highways like U.S. 30.

In the spring when the frost went out, "the bottom would drop right out" of U.S. 30. Long stretches, 40 rods or so, looked like disaster areas. They would be rutted, axle deep, with potholes full of old fence posts, gunnysacks, and other foreign material which desperate motorists had thrown under their helplessly spinning wheels.

22

Nearby farmers could make a tidy little sum pulling cars out of the holes for a dollar a throw. But eventually they grew weary of so much business and tried to ignore the whole problem.

Some of the worst areas would be "planked." The Highway Commission would lay planks, not all over the road, but just in the wheel tracks. It took careful driving and woe to you if you slipped off. During those spells I rode a horse or drove a buggy to school, about 5 miles from north of Ralston to Glidden.

PART TWO

HARD TIMES

Mark Twain Said He Didn't Know; I Did

MARK TWAIN OBSERVED he and his family were poor when he was growing up but that he didn't know it. Everyone was poor and hard times were accepted as a way of life.

We were poor, and I *did* know it!

Dad and Mother were going through that classic climax of hard times on the farm—foreclosure—but without the actual sheriff's sale finale. It amounted to the same thing inasmuch as they "lost their farm."

After World War I many Iowans migrated to the Dakotas and Minnesota. I don't know why. Dad and Mother were caught up in the movement, but they ended up in St. Croix Falls, Wisconsin, 50 miles north of Minneapolis–St. Paul on the Wisconsin border.

It was a sad but also happy move. Happy in that it was a great new experience; the beauty of that area with its rivers, lakes, and woods left a lasting impression on the family. There, a family that had known the corn-hog-cattle routine of Iowa was thrown into a wooded area where we cut saw logs in the winter and raised cattle and sheep. We had the only herd of purebred Angus cattle in the whole area. (They were almost conversation pieces in the community.) We kept our sheep within bounds with brush fences.

We enjoyed Wisconsin and I remember crying when we left because we were going back to Iowa "where the wind always blew." That emotion, I am sure, reflected Mother's attitude for I was only 8 years old and obviously not overly concerned about how much or how little the wind blew.

25

But the move *to* Wisconsin was sad, too. Dad had farmed the old Hamilton place in Carroll County for 8 or 10 years, part of them during World War I from which he was exempt as a farmer. From somewhere I have the impression that he and Mother had accumulated $20,000 which was a pretty fair piece of change for a young farmer in those days.

Then there was the small herd of Angus. They were Dad's pride and joy and continued to be during all his farming years. The plan was to buy this unimproved piece of land in Wisconsin and pay for the new buildings to be erected with the sale of pure-bred breeding stock.

But after the war in the early twenties the "bottom dropped out of things." Purebred stock sold for beef prices; all farm prices declined sharply. Dad had built a really fine set of buildings on the Wisconsin land—a big barn, silo, sheep shed, and a large modern house. But he was overextended. I was only in the 5–8-year-old range at that time and didn't realize the course of events. To get back to Iowa and to more familiar farming practices, Dad came up with an arrangement to "trade" whatever equity he had in the Wisconsin place for a farm in Clay County, Iowa—12 miles west of Spencer.

Exactly what took place in this trade operation I don't know. But after two years in Clay County we moved back to Glidden without title to either the Wisconsin farm or the Clay County farm. We had "lost a farm."

Those words are easily said. But losing a farm is a traumatic experience; it leaves its mark on a family. Many small businesses fail, of course. But the loss of a farm means not only the business and a lifetime of savings but also the home itself—the very house in which the family lives. Many families never recover from the psychological shock.

The worst of those experiences, of course, came when the sheriff, representing the eastern insurance company, forced the issue and the family's farm, goods, and chattels were put up for auction at a foreclosure sale. I give my parents much credit for handling this situation gracefully and with good sense. They signed away their equity in real estate, kept their stock and machinery, and simply "started over." Late in the twenties, Dad would shake his head at the farmer who was slaving away attempting to pay off a mortgage of perhaps $200 an acre for land then not worth more than half that figure.

"Why doesn't he let it go and start over?" he would ask.

The low point in this whole period of hard times which lasted literally from the time I was 7–8 years old until World War II, was when we packed up and moved back to Glidden. I remember Mother telling of an encounter with a Glidden storekeeper who, observing her back in the community from which she had moved a half-dozen years earlier, made some remark which indicated an assumption on his part that the family was pretty near destitute.

She assured him—to his surprise as she told it—that indeed the family was not without resources, that "we had five full freight carloads of livestock and equipment" when we came back to the point of beginning. And no doubt that was all there was; working capital was indeed minimal.

But beginning in Clay County, where Dad and Mother picked corn because we couldn't afford to hire help, where we burned old ties in a stove without legs, where Christmas was fruit and cookies and a book to read out loud, I—unlike Mark Twain—became aware that our family was going through very tough times, even though the subject as such was never discussed in the presence of the children.

I became more and more aware that both Dad and Mother were sacrificing and skimping and going without. Mother would make underskirts out of feed sacks. There was no money, none, spent on anything but necessities. One old car was traded for another old car and the purchase of the first new car was long debated—and what an event!

This whole feeling came to me through osmosis for, as I said, no words of complaint were ever spoken. No one lashed out at "the government" or took it out on Wall Street or the money-lenders. But I knew we were having hard times—and indeed we, and most farmers, were having it very tough throughout all of my growing up years.

The family was having its own private depression even before the Depression of the thirties. I recall the black headlines of the stock market crash. Dad observed, "That thing can have quite an impact out here in the country." How right he was.

Yet he never accepted the fact that there was any way out of hard times except hard work. When Calvin Coolidge vetoed the old McNary-Haugen farm bill, he allowed that "it probably was a good thing." And he knew that the New Deal palliatives were

27

only putting off the evil day; eventually we "had to get this thing on a sound footing."

Mother would never buy a thing she could bake, make, sew, or raise. Dad would rebuild a barn and use the nails he saved and straightened as he went along.

And yet he bought "good" cattle to feed and good horses to drive. That was different. You needed them. And he would drive to neighboring farms with me and we would long study a prospective 4-H calf to purchase. Typically we might pay, if we didn't have one of our own, about $50 for a calf. I would pay for that out of my own checking account. For my records I would keep careful track of feed costs for the 4-H reports. But in the end I did not pay Dad for the feed.

As a result, when it came time to go to college, I had $500 in the bank. Occasionally I would get a letter from Mother (we exchanged letters every week for years) that would have a dollar bill enclosed. I can still recall a letter from Granddad Heaton that had a $5 bill tucked in the envelope. What a big deal!

Of course, the first year in college (1931) my board and room cost $7 per week and tuition was $26 per quarter. Still, stretching $500 over the years 1931–1936 took a little doing.

But hard times were the best thing that ever happened to me. Nothing has ever really been difficult since then. And actually I had a lot of fun during those times, particularly in college. Even so, hard times are better in retrospect than in actuality.

Depression and Foreclosure Leave Their Marks

WHEN WE LIVED in Clay County, Iowa, our family was probably at its lowest point, financially and psychologically, one condition of course directly related to the other.

Whether we knew it ahead of time I don't know, but the move put our family down squarely in the middle of a community made up (with a single exception) of German-born or first-generation Germans. German was spoken in the homes. Many persons of my parents' age spoke English rather reluctantly.

28

This, of course, was not an unusual situation. Iowa was dotted with communities almost solidly made up of northern European groups, speaking their own language, following their old-country customs, doing their own thing. We just happened to settle in one.

We were not quickly accepted. I have heard Mother say that it was a year before she was in a neighbor's home. They were not basically unfriendly; they were simply clannish. So we were alone in "foreign" surroundings. And "losing out."

Four instances stand out in that brief, unhappy period that highlighted "tough times."

Miraculously the house had electricity. The power line just happened to go down our road and how it came about that the power company lighted that farm I do not know. But the house had nothing else in the way of modern conveniences.

For heat Dad bought a stove at a farm sale. It was cheap because it had no legs. It was fired from the end; you opened the door and gave the fuel a heave. The fuel during those dismal winters was railroad ties. A branch of the Rock Island cut a corner of the farm and Dad would quickly pick up old ties as soon as the section crew removed them. There was no handy-dandy chain saw to reduce those ties to firewood length. So the last thing in the evening, after the milking was done and we were ready to go into the house for supper, Dad would stop and "buck up" enough ties to last through the night. That meant taking a buck saw—one man style—and working through those old oak ties, ingrained with years' accumulation of gravel and cinders. It was slow going and terribly hard work. My job was to stand there waiting for the chunk to drop and then carry it into the house. I can still remember that as being one of the coldest experiences of my life, as every night the darkness came and the cold crowded into every crack and crevice.

That stove and the ties gave us great excitement one morning, and a great scare. To drive the night's chill out of the house, the stove would be fired up good and high as soon at possible in the morning: the hotter the better.

On that one morning, in an effort to get still more response from the legless stove (it was sitting on bricks) Dad gave a tie a heave into the firebox and knocked the whole shebang off the bricks. There it was, near red-hot, over on its side on the living room floor, the stovepipe hanging limply from the wall while

29

smoke and hot coals pushed out of the door and the smoke outlet. It was frightening, but in some way the crisis was survived as were so many others.

I remember Christmases too. Poor and among strangers we didn't jump in a car and run off to visit friends or relatives "for the holiday."

Our main Christmas presents, at least one year, were oranges and a book on the life of "Buffalo Bill" Cody. It seems to me as though both came in a box from Sears and Roebuck, although in those days getting the oranges there without freezing seems unlikely. Anyway, I remember the oranges and also that Dad read the book aloud to us at night. He liked western stories and, as I recall, a surprising amount of reading aloud was done during those times.

Two other recollections have to do with farming and the grinding hardship of it.

Along about 1922 I remember the discussions of the going rate for a man to help pick corn—by hand, of course. It seems it was 5 cents a bushel, although that sounds high because a man could make maybe as much as $4 or $5 a day.

Anyway, Dad and Mother decided that the going price was just too high; they would pick the corn themselves. They did. At daylight they would be heading for the field, the wagon bouncing over the frozen ground. Dad would pick two inside rows next the wagon, and Mother would pick the outside row. (Once she let fly with an ear of corn which hit Dad square on the nose on its way to the wagon. His nose was broken, they realized later. But they didn't stop.)

At noon they came to the house. Mother would have to start the fire in a house grown cold during the morning. Dad would shovel off the load they had picked, working off the back of the wagon and throwing each scoopful as high over his head as he could heave it into the crib. After a quick lunch they were back to the field where they stayed until as near dark as possible. They would still be out there when we got home from school. Dad would do chores, eat supper, and then go out to scoop off that last load of corn. I would hear that operation as I was going to sleep.

That memory will be with me always and be a dark cloud over any recollections of "the good old days on the farm."

The only concession my mother made during those days of corn picking was to have me buy bread during lunchtime while I

30

was in school. That expenditure worried her but she saw no other way. And I still remember with a pang of conscience her gentle reproval when she was going over the bill from the grocery and found I had charged candy on several occasions when I bought the bread. That candy, in large paper squares, I still remember. It is a bitter memory, sweet as it was at the time.

And finally the harrow cart. The drag or four-section harrow was pulled by four horses hitched abreast. The driver walked behind the drag and it was miserable walking. If it were "breaking stalks" the ground was rough and covered with trash. If the ground had been plowed the soil was loose and walking all day long was a bone-wearying exercise. Sometimes the driver would ride a horse behind the drag, while he drove the four horses pulling the rig.

After long family debate and I am sure misgivings on the part of Dad that this was something that he could "get along without," we bought a harrow cart. This was nothing but a simple, two-wheeled sulky that attached to the drag and provided transportation for the driver. The investment couldn't have been much. But it wasn't an absolute necessity. Thus it was a decision of consequence. I remember the cart very well and the slight alteration we had to make in it because it was a little too high for my Dad's not very long legs.

Once Burned Is Enough; Always Pay Cash

DAD AND MOTHER FARMED a lifetime. They retired at age 60 somewhat earlier than Dad really wanted to. But they were living on a rented farm and as help became more of a problem Dad feared the spring might come when he couldn't handle the operation and also couldn't obtain help.

Toward the end of their farming careers, both Dad and Mother were the recipients of very modest inheritances. That situation, coupled with the improved farm prices of World War II, made it possible for each of them to buy a parcel of land in Greene County. But it was too late in their lives to move onto the land they had bought. So they ended up as both renters and land-lords.

Irony was that it was probably the wartime prices of the 1914–1918 period that made it possible for them to acquire ownership in the first instance. It was not until World War II that they again became landowners and reasonably comfortable. The parcels they were able to acquire, the standard "quarter section," were too small by at least half to be a feasible operation by the time they were able to buy. There would be no buying on credit for them though. The idea of debt, any kind, was not a thought they could bear. Farm real estate taxes in Iowa were and are due in March and October, a half each time. But typically the auditor would have the assessments figured in January. The next day after Dad heard "taxes are ready" he would be there with check-book in hand, paying not just half but the whole year's assess-ments. Once paid they could be forgotten!

Working to Make a Dollar or Two

I DON'T KNOW when the imposition of a poll tax was lifted in Iowa but I am sure it prevailed well into the twenties and at the rate of $2 or $3 if I recall correctly. Farmers, at least, had the alternative of "working their poll tax." Dad always worked his because a day's work for a man with a team was an easy way to make or save $2.

Choosing some day after the corn was laid by in the summer, he got in touch with the township trustee. From him he borrowed a set of dump planks. Dump planks were a set of loose planks that would fit together on the running gears of a farm wagon and make a loose box about a foot high. With this arrangement, Dad would drive off to a neighboring pit, throw on a load of gravel or sand and take it to some spot in a township road designated by the trustee for maintenance or repair.

How this was all recorded for the worker's benefit, I do not know. It was all pretty informal. It was a total charade since the dab of sand or gravel dumped in some pothole on some county road could hardly be recognized as making much contribution to the state's Good Roads program. But the process satisfied justice—in its way. And it was worth $2!

Another episode shows the great need for cash in these times.

Granddad Heaton's creamery burned down in Glidden. He was a New York State buttermaker and knew little of farming. Yet he bought—how I don't know—a river-bottom farm, 10 miles northeast of Glidden, 18 miles north and east of Carroll.

It was a poor farm: sandy soil that burned out with the first hot weather. The house was a shack that had to be replaced, a task Granddad undertook himself. Mother would say, as she thought compassionately of her father, "Everything he did was so hard for him because he knew so little about farming." And particularly under those conditions. You couldn't jump in the pickup and run into the county seat for a little "off-farm labor."

Instead Granddad cut firewood. He cut it by hand and no doubt sawed it up into firewood length by hand. Then in the wintertime he would hitch up a team and wagon, throw on a load of wood and haul it to Carroll—a more than 30-mile round trip— where he would sell it for maybe $2 or $3!

The trip began before daylight. Granddad would fortify himself with pancakes for breakfast and take along cold pancakes to eat on the way. There were no McDonalds on that route. He would get home after dark. But he would have $2 or $3 in his pocket.

His reward amounted to a few pennies per hour for all his grueling labor during hours of darkness, cold, and snow!

33

PART THREE YOU DIDN'T JUST

PUSH A BUTTON

Wash Day

WATER as such was not such a precious commodity. But warm water was, and warm soft water was very dear.

Most farms had a cistern, a jug-shaped hole, maybe 10 feet deep and 6 feet or so wide, lined with brick and cement. Through proper arrangement of gutters and downspouts, the water off the house roof ran into the cistern. The water had as much foreign material as you might expect but it was soft! You pumped it out a pailful at a time for washing the clothes. Of course, at times you ran out; the cistern was dry. And at all times it took a lot of "blueing" to make the clothes white.

To piece out the cistern supply, you might put a few rain barrels next to the cob house where they would catch the runoff of the roof. As the summer went on these barrels would occasionally attract a bird or two, drowned, that is. And it would develop some "pollywogs" (mosquito larvae).

But the water was soft.

Hard water you could "break" with lye or wood ashes. But still we did a lot of hand-washing with hard water, frequently not warm. Hands would chap and crack. I can well remember that my wrists, just where mittens and sleeves were supposed to but didn't quite meet, would actually break open and bleed a little.

Wash day was Monday, never any other. The water was heated in a wash boiler, of the kind that are now polished and made into magazine holders. As the water was heating some

35

lye was added. This was called "breaking it." The lye brought a scum to the surface which had to be skimmed off before use.

The water was then poured into a tub, some homemade soap added, and you were ready to wash. It was as simple—and back-breaking—as taking the clothes, a piece at a time, and rubbing them against the "washboard." Or as a beginning there was a funnel-shaped, metal gadget with a long handle which could be used to give the whole operation a churning motion, up-and-down, up-and-down, water splashing over the floor and your feet. After that came the rinsing process in another tub of water. After that an attempt to wring by hand.

Later came a most remarkable advance—a round, wooden tub-like affair into which the water, soap, and clothes could be placed and actually agitated mechanically with the power of a gas engine or, later, an electric motor. And then, of all things, the "double tub era." Two tubs, side by side, one for washing, the other for rinsing, with a wringer mounted between. Feeding the clothes through the wringer, first from the washtub and then

COURTESY ISU HISTORY COLLECTION

from the rinse tub, was a hand job and dangerous. After years and years of admonishing us kids to be careful, and of being careful herself, Mother let her hand get pulled into the wringer with understandably painful results which handicapped her for years.

Of course, there was still this small matter of drying the clothes. Even after wringing they were heavy with water. If it were at all feasible, as during the summer and early spring and late fall, they went on the line, of course. But on some bitter winter days I have seen Mother, hands numb with cold, hanging out a wash that would freeze stiff almost as soon as she hung it.

The alternative was to put it on clothes racks in the house or hang it on ropes strung across the rooms or over the backs of chairs. Whereupon the windows steamed over, the walls got moist, everything would get wet, clammy, and cold, and the whole house would smell like a commercial laundry.

I well remember an accident resulting from a laundry arrangement of the olden days. I was perhaps 3. The washing machine was out in the backyard. It was powered with a hand-cranked gas engine, one that was wheeled in on wash day and out to do some other farm chore another day. As Mother went around to crank the engine—often a process that defeated males—I investigated some of the washing machine's exposed gears. Mash! The scar on my right-hand finger remains to this day.

What Happened to All These Necessities?

ARGO STARCH . . . mothballs . . . carpet beaters . . . curtain stretchers . . . soapstones . . . flatirons. Those and dozens of other household items left in no time at all. "Spring housecleaning" also vanished.

Soapstones saved us in those upstairs unheated bedrooms that were just one shade warmer than the whole outdoors. It took real courage to go up and jump into bed when it was 10 below outside. Usually we did just that, but it was a mighty fast process. When Mother did feel sorry for us, or if we were ailing, we used a soapstone. It was about the dimension of a thick board, perhaps 10 inches long and 6 inches wide, had a bail attached to one end and a very smooth surface. We would heat the stone on the cookstove and slide it down under the covers. How good it felt!

Others used flatirons—the kind you did the ironing with. You now see them used for doorstops. We had several at our house. When we were using them for their designed purpose they were heated on the cookstove, two heating while one was in use. When all was ready, the item sprinkled and with just the right amount of starch, a heated iron would be grabbed off the stove with a potholder, rubbed quickly over an open mail-order catalog to be sure it was clean and also to be certain it was not too hot, and then applied to the job at hand. When that iron cooled off, it was exchanged for another.

Mother always said she ironed with one hand and poured cobs in the cookstove with the other.

Starch . . . you weren't really dressed unless your shirt was starched all over and then double starched at the collar and cuffs. Were they stiff and did they cut? You bet. Of course dresses and aprons had the starch treatment, too—but only lightly.

I have seen mother take a great pile of clothes, many of them starched, and, with a pan full of water, hand sprinkle each item, roll it into a ball, and tuck it into a clothes basket. The basket would be crammed full. That would be the next morning's ironing. All morning.

I wonder how many hundreds of shirts I sent home in laundry bags while I was away at college. Many, I know. They would come back all nicely washed and ironed and frequently with some cookies tucked in one corner of the bag. I have seen a mail truck pull away from the ISU campus office with a full load of laundry bags. All homeward bound.

Mothballs? Now you buy them, I believe, to keep rabbits out of the garden. In the spring all winter clothes were packed away with mothballs tucked in pockets and containers. Mothballs did have a pretty distinctive aroma that stayed stubbornly with winter clothes during the first few fall wearings!

A Baby! With No Running Water?

A STANDARD JOKE has been built around the suggestion that the single most important thing to do in preparing for a birth in the olden days was to "boil the water." Just what purpose this activity served has been lost for many years.

But if the young mother wants to try to turn her mind back to an earlier day, she might consider looking after her little bundle for a day or two without running water, or even any warm water except that heated on a cookstove, and, worst of all, without cleansing tissue, an absolute necessity for both ends!

At the turn of the century, the need for a doctor at time of birth was not an essential; a couple of neighbor women would fill the bill. Maternity clothes hadn't been invented; pregnant women just stayed home. And of course jolting across the ruts in a buggy didn't encourage travel in any case.

39

Following delivery, the mother might stay in bed for two weeks, probably the nearest thing to a vacation she would ever get.

Summer or winter, the newborn baby was immediately dressed in wool. Bare feet were never seen. Socks were pinned to the diaper. And in summer or winter, the baby's head had to be covered. I am informed that my face was carefully covered with a silk scarf for some time, even during the mildest and warmest of summer days.

Also a wool band was wrapped around the baby's navel and pinned as tightly as possible. Clearly baby was protected, both ends and the middle.

Except under the most unusual circumstances, all babies were breast fed and for considerable periods. It was reliably reported that my father's youngest brother, the "baby" of the family of six, nursed until he was quite ambulatory.

These few paragraphs are a rather lighthearted and casual commentary on at least one of life's greatest moments—being born. But they in no way try to reflect the suffering and the tragedy of the times of those early settlers when so many mothers died in childbirth.

The Kitchen Range: Heart of Everything

THE KITCHEN RANGE was the heart of the house. It was heat. It was for cooking. It was hot water. It was for drying wet mittens and soggy overshoes. It was for baking. It was for souring the milk that would turn into cottage cheese. It was for warming the shivering, newborn lamb or pig. It was for sitting around, with feet ranged around the open oven door.

The kitchen range was the last thing to be taken down and carried out to the wagon when it was moving time. It was the first thing to be set up. There could be no living in a house until the kitchen range was going.

The range had many parts. The fire, of course, was all con-

40

he Advance Windsor—Ward's Old Reliable

Easy Monthly Payments

$5.00 Down

$5.00 a Month

Order Blank on Page 504

Popular for Many Years

There may be more attractive ranges in this catalogue than the **Advance Windsor,** but there are none of better quality or which will give longer, more satisfactory service. It has been on the market for many years, during which time it has proved its worth to thousands of housewives. We guarantee it to please **you** and fulfill **your** stove requirements in every way.

The **Advance** is built of large heavy castings, carefully fitted by hand. Every part is ground so that it goes into place easily, without being forced, and the body is cemented and bolted together so tightly that there are no heat-wasting leaks. This is why the **Advance** uses so little fuel, despite its large size and huge cooking capacity.

Oven.—Unusually big and roomy—20 inches square. Bakes perfectly in every corner and will not warp or get out of shape. Steel lined cast iron drop door with accurate heat register.

Cooking Top.—Very large. Extra heavy combination 8 and 9-inch lids; two cyclonic, one sectional and three plain lids. The cyclonic lids save considerable fuel. Can be furnished with highly polished top that requires no blacking. See table.

Fire Box.—Size for coal, 18 by 8 by 5 inches. With the end linings removed, it takes 21-inch wood. Burns absolutely any kind of fuel because it is equipped with a duplex grate; one side for coal, other side for wood. Will be replaced if it burns out within 10 years.

Reservoir.—Made large and serviceable like the rest of the range; holds 28 quarts. Heats by contact. Hand made of heavy pure copper, tinned on the inside. Will not rust.

High Closet.—Nickel plated bands, brackets, nameplate, door handle and back guard corners. The high closet is large and commodious and is closed by a balanced roll steel door.

Shelf.—Handy shelf, 34 inches long and 6 inches wide, between high closet and cooking top. White enamel splasher strip underneath shelf.

Towel Bar.—Nickeled towel bar across front of stove.

Water Front. For heating water in range boiler. Shipping weight, 17 pounds.
1 68 C 462—Add................$5.50

Patented Cyclonic Lid Saves Heat

Style of Top	Number with Reservoir and High Closet	Price with Reservoir and High Closet Cash	Time	Number with High Closet, No Reservoir
Plain	268 C 436	$61.25	$68.25	268 C 435
Polished	268 C 434	62.75	69.75	268 C 433

Prices and Dimensions of Advance Windsor

Price with High Closet, No Reservoir Cash	Time	Extreme Height	Height to Top	Size of Oven Inches Width	Depth	Height	Size of Top with Reservoir	Size of Top without Reservoir	Shipping Weight with Reservoir	Shipping Weight without Reservoir
$56.25	$63.25	62 in.	31 in.	20	20	13	48x25½ in.	42x25½ in.	660 pounds	600 pounds
57.75	64.75	62 in.	31 in.	20	20	13	48x25½ in.	42x25½ in.	660 pounds	600 pounds

COURTESY ISU HISTORY COLLECTION

centrated at one side, built over a grate, the shaking of which each morning marked the official start of a new day. There was the warming oven, up behind the stove. This was for drying mittens or keeping food reasonably warm after it left the stove. Then there was the oven itself, beside the firebox, much in the proportions of your modern range oven.

And then still beyond the oven was the reservoir. This was a water-tight unit, holding perhaps a couple of pails of water. Usually the water, after a reasonable period of cooking, was tepid to warm. A little tepid to warm water was a pleasant thing to have in those days when the idea of a flood of hot water out of a faucet was beyond dreams.

Many a little lamb or pig, fresh-born and perhaps rejected by its mother, would be coaxed into life by the kitchen stove. Usually in a basket with a gunnysack for "his blanket."

41

Mother used to speculate on how many tons of cobs she had burned in her lifetime. Besides quantities of cobs, some wood, a little coal. Coal had to be bought. But a cob fire needed constant attention. It was roaring-hot one minute, a bed of coals the next. Run to the cob house with the basket; pour in another pailful; adjust the damper in the stovepipe; close the draft. And then repeat the process.

All that notwithstanding, life revolved around the cookstove. At night we would open up the oven door and everyone would try to get nearby, or get their feet on the open door and settle down with their books, papers, or schoolwork. Or else spread out on the oilcloth on the kitchen table.

In those winter days, when little was to be accomplished except chores morning and night, just a lot of time was spent around that open oven door. A lot of things got settled there.

I mentioned oilcloth on the kitchen table. That was standard and a new piece of oilcloth was a bit of an event.

The oilcloth on the table served a special use. Mother was tutoring me for a spelling bee. She would pronounce the words and I would write them on the oilcloth. Dozens and dozens of words would fill the kitchen table. I seemed to learn better that way, seeing them and hearing them at the same time. When the table was full, Mother would take the washcloth and wipe it clean. And we could start over.

We frequently washed dishes at the kitchen stove. It kept the dishwater hot. And since the water was hard, it had to be hot. I can remember Mother washing dishes as either Alice or I dried them. Came the pots and pans, she would scrape them with an old putty knife and work on the most resistant spots with her fingernails. The nails on her right hand were always worn down from friction on those stubborn spots.

The Water Jug: Now Another Antique Item

AN EARLY SPRING assignment was to cover the water jug, an ordinary gallon jug of crockery, the kind you now see selling for some outrageous price in antique shops.

Dad would hunt up a burlap sack and carefully wrap the jug so that it was covered with several layers up to and around the neck. Binder twine, crisscrossed every which way, held the burlap.

43

Then you went to the cob pile and found a cob that just fit for a cork and your summer "thermos bottle" was ready.

The last thing you did before starting for the field was to fill the jug at the pump or hydrant, wherever the water was the coldest. Then you immersed the whole jug in the tank, soaking the burlap completely. The strap through the handle of the jug was then slipped over the hame on the collar of the harness and you were on your way, as your "coffee break" sloshed along on the old mare's shoulder and the burlap dripped down her foreleg.

Once in the field the jug was set by a post, tucked back under some fence row weeds or covered with your jacket. By noon or night, on hot days, the water would be about the temperature of bath water.

But that thermos effect was remarkably effective and what a wonderfully refreshing thing it was to pull up at the end of the row, hunt up that jug, swing it up over your arm and—one handed —let its cool contents kill the cotton that had been building up in your throat. I can still hear that old jug gurgle. Forgetting the jug and leaving it in the field at noon or night was not something to be taken lightly or soon forgotten—again.

We Really Appreciated Cold Milk

THE OLD HAMILTON FARM where I was born 10 miles northeast of Glidden was unmodern in every respect. It was just a big, old, square house that Granddad Hamilton had built when he moved to Iowa in the 1880s: no electricity; no running water. It had the usual path to the privy. It did have an icehouse that was filled from the river during the winter.

The old icehouse was filled with ice sawed from the river. It was packed in sawdust and carried into the refrigerator in the kitchen during the summer months. But we moved and for years and years were without any form of refrigeration—other than nature's!

44

So for the butter, cream, and milk, we sought out the coolest place we could think of to keep it. That was the sump around the well. This was a hole, usually bricked up, some 6 feet deep and 4 feet across, surrounding the well at the windmill. It was covered with planks, laid loose. So the butter, the milk, and the cream, in such containers as were needed, were lowered on a rope into the sump. When the plank was replaced, you had shut the door on your refrigerator.

Before a meal you went out to the well, pulled back the plank, and brought your victuals to the surface. Refrigerated they were not. I remember the butter frequently had the consistency of cream when it came to the surface.

In Glidden, at both grandparents', things were very modern; they had iceboxes. The milk was always cold and the butter solid. But best of all they had the ice man. On those occasions when I was in town during the summer, I joined the rest of the neighborhood kids in following the ice wagon and grabbing at any slivers or chunks of ice that fell to the ground as he chipped out a 25, 30, or 40 pound chunk to fill the box. Ice was a luxury. What did that make homemade ice cream?

Food: We Supplied It All

ALICE HAMILTON WALTERS WRITES . . .

IN THE COUNTRY, if you didn't grow vegetables you didn't have them. Lettuce and celery were unknown in the winter. Rhubarb in the spring was a welcome change from apples as the only fresh fruit throughout the winter.

Tomatoes were the only vegetable canned until something called cold packing came into use. Root vegetables—potatoes, carrots, and turnips—could be stored in caves under certain conditions. Cabbage was sometimes stored in a pit lined with paper or straw and covered with dirt. On a warmer day with some thaw, a head could be pried loose for use.

45

Of course another way to preserve cabbage was in the form of kraut, usually concocted—smell and all—in large stone jars, 10-gallon size.

Water glass had a good deal to do with food preparation in the olden days. It was the way you kept eggs, accumulated in the fall before the old hens quit laying, for winter use. You placed the eggs in a large stone jar and covered them with a jelly-like substance known as water glass. It kept the air away from the eggs and although they were hardly grade A after a couple months of such treatment they could still be used for baking. For years we "put down" eggs in water glass.

Beef was only butchered in the winter when it could be used fresh. Later it was canned in the oven. The chunks of meat were placed in glass jars; these were set in pans of water in the oven for several hours to complete the cooking. Low temperatures were necessary.

Pork butchered in the spring was salted. A brine of salt, sugar, and saltpeter was prepared. The meat was stored in a large stone jar. After a period of time it might be smoked. The loin was sliced, fried, and "put down in lard." This meant cooking the meat, placing it in a jar, and covering it with melted lard. Sausage was treated the same.

Sausage was made by grinding all the "scrappy" bits and then seasoning a dishpan full at one time. When it was mixed a trial patty was cooked to be sure of the seasoning. Some was eaten fresh. The rest was stored in lard. Lard was made by stripping out the fat as the hog was cut up. Then the fat was either cut into small pieces or coarsely ground. Usually Mother cooked this in the oven long enough for most of the fat to melt. She used the potato ricer to press the lard out of the "cracklings." The hot liquid fat was strained through a cloth to remove the crumbs of cracklings. The lard was stored in covered containers. Cracklings went into soap.

A piece of the rind (skin) of ham or side meat was used (fat side down) to rub over the griddle to keep pancakes from sticking.

After the pork was gone in the summer, the only meat was either beef purchased at the butcher shop or chickens. Chickens, for both meat and eggs, were a product of most small-town and farm families. Mother took eggs, cream, butter, or cottage cheese to town and brought home flour in 49-pound cloth bags, sugar in 100-pound muslin bags inside burlap bags, salt in cloth bags, baking powder, soda, dried fruit in the winter, some laundry soap

46

(Procter & Gamble, P&G, in bars). Occasionally bananas were on the list. For baking bread yeast foam was used. This was a form of dry yeast in cakes about 1 inch square and ½ inch thick. The noon before baking day the yeast was put to soak in warm water. When it had softened about suppertime some flour was added. When this got bubbly all the rest of the liquid was added and enough flour to make a stiff batter. This then sat beside the stove to keep warm until morning. The bread was usually completed the following afternoon. This yeast did not need refrigeration but it was slow.

Baker's bread came to Glidden in the 1880s or 1890s. In the 1920s, three one-pound loaves sold for 25 cents.

You Can Trade If You Don't Have Cash

MOTHER always went to town to "do her trading," and she traded eggs and cream for groceries for many years during hard times.

But it worked the other way, too. Peddlers and salesmen who came farm-to-farm were willing to do some trading to get business.

Farm magazine subscription salesmen would drive in with a chicken crate tied onto their car and would help us run down, if it were necessary, a few old hens which they would take in exchange for a year's subscription.

So Your Waffle Iron Sticks Occasionally?

A MODERN WAFFLE IRON has been designed for beauty and merchandising by Madison Avenue and engineers have equipped it with lights and bells so that even a novice cook can almost always bring off a product that meets with reasonable satisfaction. Try this then.

47

Take an old-fashioned cookstove fired with corncobs which give off a quick blast of heat and then subside into a cupful of ashes.

To take full advantage of those quick bursts of flame you remove the stove lid so that the old black waffle iron is right over the flame. You cook one side, by guess and by golly. When you assume it is done you flip the iron over and expose the other side to the flames which are by then beginning to subside.

Of course, adding interest to the operation is the fact that the wooden handles on the iron have long ago been burned off and replaced with material at hand—naturally corncobs. They are stuck quite uncertainly on the iron spindles that remain. No lights to flash; no bells to ring. Only Mother's intuition as to when they were done.

How Mother ever brought off that operation I will never know. And why she was willing to do it as often as she did, under those circumstances, I will also never know. But I will always be grateful! Mother reminds me that her recipe called for three eggs and that the irons had to be greased for each waffle.

The Rawleigh Man Came with Horse and Buggy

ACTUALLY there were two—the Rawleigh man and the Watkins man. They were the early-day version of the Avon lady, except they peddled spices, salves, patent medicines, cough syrup, and painkiller. (I understand they still operate in some areas.)

Naturally, they came originally with a horse-drawn rig. They would pull up at the back door, tie their horse, and bring in their cases packed full of the popular needs of those times. They were always welcome and Mother usually bought. As a matter of fact she would have a list waiting "until the next time the Rawleigh man comes around." She thought his spices were superior to those in town.

But the most popular item was a salve especially prepared for sore udders. This came in a distinctive round container, 3 or 4 inches across and 2 inches deep. It must have been a full pound or more. A box was always kept down at the cattle barn where we did the milking and it was used in great quantities on teats that were chapped or cracked. Another box was at the horse barn where it was handy for sore necks or any other abrasion. A box was at the house too and it was the standard hand lotion for the whole family. Its odor was distinctive; no money had been wasted on milady's favorite scent. It was very hard, but once applied to hands and chapped wrists it produced a protective coating almost like another pair of mittens. It would last about as long. At corn picking time, men with hands and wrists raw and cracked from the cold, the wet, and the abrasiveness of dry cornstalks would rub on vast quantities of Rawleigh's udder salve both night and morning.

Gray Stoneware
Butter Churns

$2 48

Glazed inside and out. Stoneware cover. Dasher made of hard maple. Length of handle, 3½ feet.

Waffle Irons.

No. 16096. The American Waffle Iron. Simple in construction, convenient to handle, easy to clean.

Size, No......... 8   9
Each............$0.65 .68

$1 19

Cold Blast Oil Lantern
Burns 40 Hours on One
Filling

**Majestic Bread
Maker**

Small Size
Kneads
From 2 to
6 Loaves

$2 60

The easiest, quickest and surest way of preparing perfect bread. The Majestic entirely does away with long and tiresome hand kneading. Two to ten loaves are thoroughly kneaded in about three minutes. The work is done with scientific accuracy, thoroughly and evenly, producing bread that is firm, light, white and free from unbroken starch cells.

49

PART FOUR   THRESHING

AND SUCH

Horsepower, But Also a Part of the Family

PEARL AND LAURA, Dick and Darby, Old Buck, Ed and Kate, Bill and Jake, King, Old Pete, Beauty, and on and on.

We had quite a time selecting names for our kids as they came along. Each suggestion had already been preempted by a horse that was a part of the family at one time.

Dad kept twelve head of horses, enough to run two two-bottom "gang" plows. Harnessing up six head of horses, three abreast, and getting them properly hitched was no small assignment; the horses needed to be well broken and the driver well trained. But when he had a fistful of lines in hand, shouted "giddap," and the plow bit into the loam and began to turn over the rich black soil, a great feeling of power hit the man on that plow seat. He had a sense of some accomplishment, like the man who insists on driving a stick shift car because he wants to feel he is part of the car's power.

Always there were a few regulars, the tried and true, the leaders. These were the "lead team." They set the pace. A colt just being broken was put somewhere in the complex so his antics could be reasonably well controlled. But no matter how veteran the teams might be, it took a skillful driver to manage six head, keeping them moving fast enough on the turns to avoid getting some horse outside of his tugs or into some tangle. Turning was an art.

Horses are like people; they are all different. Some will lead; others will follow. Some will shirk; others will overdo. Some will dominate the barn lot, driving their peers away from the water tank or the salt block. Some will kick and nip; others never.

51

Jake and Bill were the old mules. They were the hired man's team because you couldn't overheat them or overwork them. They would "look after themselves." I drove them a good deal myself. During corn cultivating, a two-mule job, they would start out strong in the morning. About 10 o'clock some alarm clock would go off in their innards and their personalities would change. As we would go back and forth across the field, they would go slower and slower as we went away from the house. But as they turned around and headed in the direction of home, all hell couldn't hold them. The lines, wrapped around your back, would cut ridges in your shoulders. That performance would go on until noon, gradually getting more and more pronounced. Same thing in the afternoon. They weren't a favorite team.

The ideal was "Dad's team," the nerviest, best disciplined, liveliest team on the farm. They were taught to drive "up on the bit." You kept a tight line on them at all times, but they kept a steady unvarying pace, heads high, and they moved as though they meant to get the job done.

Then there were the others, gentle, plodding, much-loved creatures who went out to do a day's work and if they got either themselves or their driver in any trouble, it was most unintentional. Ed and Kate were that kind. We kept them many years. But unless you were going to end up with a "barn full of old pelters," you had to be selling older horses and buying younger ones all the time. This caused pangs because they had become so much a part of the family.

When we sold old Ed it was a subject Dad wouldn't admit for a time and when it was brought up he allowed, staring straight into his plate in a way that didn't encourage response, that there came a time when economic reality (not his words) had to prevail over sentiment. It was such a touchy subject that when it came time to deliver old Ed to the horse buyer, Dad saddled up the riding horse, led Ed down the lane and took him some three miles to another farm, all after dark one night so we wouldn't have to see him go!

The buying and selling went on with some regularity. The selling usually took place with a horse buyer, a professional buyer who "drove the country" and bought for the "eastern market." We had a relative who would come out from New York State every year, stay with us, and drive around the country while he

52

picked up a carload or two of horses. They were shipped back east.

Buying a horse was, and still is, for that matter, a science. Getting a "good sound horse" at an auction took experience and a good eye. They could have "side bones," a "hip down," be "windy," be balky, be sweenied, or just plain mean. The list could go on and on. And, of course, the most elementary skill was to be able to determine a horse's age by examining its teeth.

Being "balky" meant just not wanting to pull, and *not* pulling. The phrase was "not pull the hat off your head." We got one that way once. We didn't keep it too long. But we gave it a bit of a cure, too. I remember I hitched a team to a load of shelled corn in the crib. It was no load at all, but this one horse wouldn't tighten a tug. With a determined look in his eye, Dad harnessed up another team, "his" team, brought them out, threw a log chain around the balky horse's neck, shouted "giddap" to all four head, and started out. I thought for a while that the balky horse was going to divide into two pieces: head and body. But the neck stretched only about so far when he decided that moving that load of corn was after all an idea of some merit.

We bought a kicker one time too. They are just plain dangerous; very dangerous. Dad just saddled up and took that one back to the seller. I don't know what settlement, if any, was arrived at. But we didn't want a kicker around!

Keeping horses healthy was important. They were your power, almost as important as the weather. In the spring when the horses were "soft" you were careful to start out easy. They had to be broken in. You were especially careful to avoid the sore shoulders or sore necks that developed where collars rode down on the top of the neck or up against the broadest face of the shoulder where the main pressure from the collar came to bear. As spring went on, these areas would toughen and take much punishment. But if a sore developed early in the spring it was tough to heal it up in day-in and day-out work. So great care was taken each night when the collars were taken off to scrape them thoroughly with a blunt knife. Cleaning the collars was a ritual, along with inspecting the shoulders and necks. Woe be to the hired man who neglected this. It was inevitable some sores would develop. These were carefully doctored and powdered each night and morning. Putting a collar down against a shoulder with a raw spot as big as your hand made you feel pretty mean;

but the work had to go on. Sometimes doctoring sore necks, sore shoulders, or even trimming hoofs, particularly on younger horses, would provide a bit of excitement. Not all took kindly to such attention. Whereupon you put on a "twitch." This was nothing but a foot-long stick with a 6- or 8-inch loop of small rope attached to one end. You simply reached through this loop and grabbed a handful of his upper lip and twisted this twitch in tourniquet fashion around a chunk of lip about as big as your hand. This had a remarkably calming effect on a horse. I was never sure why, but it worked.

One dread with horses, especially young ones, was having them get cut up in a fence. They would stick a foot through a fence as they reached over for a bite on the other side. They might either receive a scar that would blemish their salability or injure themselves so that they could not work for a while. A telephone line once went down in our neighbor's pasture and his horses got tangled up in it, just plain smooth wire. They started running. One horse caught the wire just in front of the hock joint. The wire shortly sawed its way into a vein of such consequence that the horse quickly bled to death.

Dad kept good horses. He kept good harness. He wanted his horses well driven. Woe be to the hired man who let the lines go slack. A team was to be "driven, not herded." And so there was a minimum of carelessness in handling Hamilton horses. That is perhaps one reason why runaways didn't occur around our place; I remember only one and it was not serious.

A runaway is an utterly frightening sight though. Picture two big horses, hitched to a wagon or a hayrack. The driver loses control. They spook and break into a dead run. They become terrorized as the wagon or whatever they are pulling begins to disintegrate and fly off in all directions. They try to run through gates, but whatever of the wagon is still intact catches on the gatepost and there is a great crash. Even more panic-stricken, they may run blindly through a fence, cutting themselves on barbed wire. One may fall, but still lashed together there is a sickening scene as they become even more entangled in the harness. If they make it to the barn, they will both try to run in a single door at the same time. Finally stopped, they are utterly winded, exhausted through exertion and fright. Their nostrils flare, their eyes reflect sheer panic. They are a sad sight, equipment and harness reduced to shreds. A runaway at any time was a near tragedy. In Depression time it was such as to cast a pall over the household not unlike that which accompanied disease in the feedyard or lightning striking a herd or a flock.

A contrast to the runaway was the performance of a really superior pulling team demonstrating its ability to "lay in there" and move the near unmovable load. Most horses were sufficiently trained to move any average load, one that began to roll with ordinary effort. But it took a well-trained, well-matched, and well-driven team that could dig in and with great coordinated effort—almost crouching, muscles bulging, dirt flying, nostrils flaring, harness creaking in an almost frightening way—finally begin to move a great load. Dad always meant to have one such team. It was his pride. It was a mark of esteem on the threshing run. And the ultimate accolade came when that team which had been putting forth this almost frightening effort stopped when he shouted "whoa"; stock-still, no nervousness. *That* was a good team.

The rapport between a man or boy and his team became very great. You knew them; they knew you. At the end of the row you stopped, got off your plow and went around to run your hand under the collars and pull out from the top of the collar any handful of mane that might have worked its way in. You might let them "blow a while" before starting another round. You could appreciate it when they were tired. You felt badly when the ground was rough and cloddy in the spring and it was tough going.

Horseflesh was terribly abused in the building of America. It was often abused on the average farm, important as its welfare was. But it was simply used up and replaced as needed as the transcontinental railroads were pushed across the prairies, much of it with horsepower. The toll must have been frightening. One of the most sickening stories I ever read was that of the Alaska Gold Rush from Skagway to the Klondike over some of the most awful mountain terrain on this continent. Horses were loaded with packs, driven until they could not take another step, shot or left to die while the feverish men pushed on. One of the parts of that now famous trail is known as Dead Horse Gulch and the story of how it came to be so named sickens any person who has ever really known a horse—as a boy did growing up on a farm in the 1920s and early thirties.

Horses were a part of our life.

Horses—Loved, Cussed, and Indispensable . . .

Turning over a 40-acre field was a long slow job with a 12- or 14-inch sulky plow. A gang for a 2-bottom plow was more common, pulled by five or six horses.

Farmers didn't need to jog for exercise after a day of walking through freshly plowed ground following a spring-toothed harrow.

Eight-horse hitches, such as this, pulling two 8-foot discs in tandem, plus a harrow, were rare.

A harrow cart—when Dad bought one it was a big decision! Harrow carts were not necessities—drivers could walk!

Spring plowing. Note the dark strips where cornstalks had been raked and burned. Poor agronomy.

Corn planting, with a wire that "checked" or dropped a hill every 40 inches, was springtime's most delicate and demanding operation.

Cultivating corn was the first real fieldwork for a farm boy; a big event that turned into a bore.

Cutting the hay, with a steady team hitched to a mower with a 5-foot sickle bar, was the easiest and most pleasant of many steps involved in the haymaking process.

The hay was cut and cured, ready to head for the barn or stack. By hand it went on the rack.

COURTESY ISU HISTORY COLLECTION

*This kind of horsepower elevated corn, powered
threshing machines, and did other similar jobs. One or
more teams, hitched to booms, plodded endlessly around
the circle while the gearbox in the center converted
horsepower to the task at hand. [below] Horses doing
fieldwork were seldom shod. But those used on streets or
roads made regular trips to the blacksmith shop. So,
too, did every farmer with any kind of machinery repair
job. The blacksmith was an important person.*

COURTESY HERB PIKE, WHITING, IOWA

*A team stands patiently as the front end of the wagonload
of ear corn is "hoisted" so that the load will slide
out the rear of the wagon and into an elevator hopper.*

61

Typical husking wagons with high bangboards. These many pickers in an after-the-snow scene were no doubt neighbors in to help finish up the picking for a farmer who had suffered some misfortune.

A stop at the watering tank was the last thing before starting to the field with the teams; the first stop upon returning to the barn at noon or night.

A rack, mounted on a bobsled, was the prescribed conveyance for hauling corn fodder from field to feedlot.

63

Old Pete and King

Two of our usual number of horses were special for a growing-up kid: Old Pete and King. Old Pete was always old. I don't know when he came onto the scene. He was a chunky little horse suitable for riding, driving on the buggy, and serving as an extra during the heavy work of spring.

His two chief characteristics seemed to work in contradiction; he was badly crippled in the shoulders, "all stove up" they called it, and he had energy without limit. He was really gentle, but hitched to any vehicle on the road or in the field it was always maintained that he never tightened a tug; he always pulled the load with the bit in his teeth. Mother would drive him on the buggy and claim "he just pulled my arms off." You couldn't slow him down.

In the spring Old Pete would be put in as an extra on a six-horse hitch, the outside horse in the lead. He was obviously in the lead. All the other horses would be 400 to 500 pounds heavier. But he made up for it in energy.

As he got older his worth became more in question. But still he was used for spring work. When it was over he was thin and tired. But he would run on grass with little to do until next spring work time. Dad would debate, although not very seriously, the fact that Old Pete ought to go to the rendering works. But he didn't have the heart to do that after Old Pete had pulled his guts out doing the spring work, nor, for that matter, after he had loafed and fattened all year. Actually, I don't know how he met his fate.

During grade school I sometimes rode him to school. My high school nickname came from him. I'm still Pete to high school classmates.

King was another story, and one with a sad ending. One year Dad went to Nebraska to buy cattle and brought back, in the same car with the calves, a classy young colt. He was saddle quality, no doubt out of a bronco mare and possibly a purebred, saddle-type sire. He weighed maybe 1,000 pounds, too light for field work, and we no longer used the buggy.

One of the hired men broke him and from then on he was my horse. We had a good deal of livestock and a farm that was a mile long with no fences. A saddle horse was valuable. And he

64

was a delight. He was a handsome little horse with plenty of nerve. I loved to ride him into town, or anywhere. He loved to run, really run.

I had two close calls with him. He was a flat-footed little cuss and had a tendency to fall when the footing was slippery. One time I was rounding up sheep after a light snow. He turned too short and fell while at a full gallop. There was no time to shake loose. So down I went with him—boy and horse sliding off across the pasture in a great cloud of snow. It was a real tumble. King was back on his feet faster than I was and fortunately I was free of the stirrups. We went on about our business—more slowly.

Earlier, when he was less well broken, I started to mount him when we were at the far side of the farm, a mile from the buildings. He spooked when I had one foot in the stirrup and was just half ready to throw the other leg across. This threw me on my stomach right across the saddle, head on one side, feet on the other. This really spooked him; he headed for the house as hard as he could run. By then I was more scared than he was. All the stories of youngsters being dragged to death by a horse when they were thrown but had one foot caught in a stirrup flashed through my mind. I still had enough wits about me to get a hold of one rein and with that began to run him in a tighter and tighter circle. He soon calmed down and stopped. But I was one scared kid.

King had a sad end. He loved to run and he loved to get the other horses running in the pasture. He was very nearly devilish in that respect. A power line ran through the pasture. One night King got the other horses running. One of them ran into a pole and snapped it off. The hot wires dropped, electrocuting King and several other workhorses.

That happened the first year I was away at college. The folks weren't going to tell me until I got home, and they didn't. But the night I got home one of the neighbors dropped in and, in the course of the conversation, expressed his sympathy to me for the loss of King. Of course, the loss of the other horses was the real financial loss to Dad. But the family mourned King.

Hired Men, Too, Were a Part of the Family

THROUGHOUT THE WINTER Dad had been keeping his eye out for a good hired man. The search had no particular science to it. You "heard about" someone, or someone had worked for a neighbor, or a neighbor boy was ready to hire out. No advertising. The word just got around, and somehow a new hired man would be slated to appear on the scene about March 1.

Some men just came down the road looking for work. If Dad needed a hand he would hire them. (Mother said he would hire anyone who came along.) One man whose name became a household word, Earl King, was one who just walked in, asked for work, and stayed four years.

Typically each spring we had a new hired man who stayed at least through threshing. They were all single men. It was taken for granted they would simply move in and become a part of the family: sharing all meals, the bathroom or the privy, reading the family newspapers, and generally, as Mother put it, "being underfoot." Part of the time I shared a bedroom with one or two hired men. Sometimes we would have two men; during corn picking, maybe three.

We had some fine men who really became almost part of the family. But they were the exception. Some were real "characters." We had several drop in asking for work who owned nothing but the clothes on their backs. One, I recall, we had to supply with a cap before he could go to work. These floaters were more likely to be the "extra hands" at rush seasons.

You can imagine those first meals when the family sat down at the table with a total stranger. Everybody eyed the new man—what he ate (Mother studied his first reactions with great concern, wondering if he was going to be a "queer eater")—and his table manners or lack of them. We had one who would fill his plate with food. Then, when the next service dish was passed to him, he would set that right down in his plate while he speared what he wanted. The oilcloth (we used nothing else) would get a little sloppy after about the third time around!

There would be the silent ones and the talkers. Dad couldn't stand the talkers. He reacted by clamming up, bolting his food, and leaving the table. Things got particularly strained if, after supper, the new man went in and plopped himself down in Dad's

66

chair, or picked up a magazine that someone had been planning to read. There was no television, no radio, just some chairs and a table with a droplight in the middle of the living room. Mother would spend a long time washing the dishes. Alice and I would likely do our homework around the kitchen table. Thus the evening would eventually pass.

Mother used to be deathly afraid that one of the hired hands would bring a "social disease" to our house. I remember once when she found some blood stains on the sheets in the hired man's bed and with great dismay pointed them out to me.

Of course, meeting Mother's standards in the general problem of cleanliness wasn't easy. There was no quick shower for the man who had been working out in the dust and wind all day. One I remember had a particularly bad problem with smelly feet. Dad threatened to pour some sheep dip in his shoes! He was finally fired but not because his feet stank. Not many were fired, although some were no doubt given hints. In some cases the work "just played out" sooner than had been expected. That is, Dad figured he would rather do it alone.

The ideal hired man was not only pleasant to have around the house, but was also good with horses, dependable, and could see things to do. The ultimate test in that respect, insofar as Dad was concerned, was the man who would see something to do on a rainy day. After a steady soaking rain during the night, the "average" man would clean out the horse barn, feed and water horses, and stand in the barn door without being able to see another single thing that could be done on that soggy morning. There was plenty, of course, and Dad soon made that plain.

Another mark of a good hired man was one who could get up without being called, who didn't need an alarm clock. The moral fiber had begun to decay in the man who had to have an alarm clock; we never had one in the house for our own use. Chores and breakfast would take until 7 when it was time to be heading for the field. With an hour out for dinner, it would be fieldwork until 6. Then supper and feed the teams. We would knock off a little early on late Saturday afternoon if we weren't too rushed. Chores to do on Sunday.

Another test was the hired man who, when he was going to be gone overnight or over the weekend, would be sure there was enough hay thrown down from the mow so that Dad or I could feed the horses without going up into the mow. There was a

67

good man! At one time "Missouri hired men" were quite common in Iowa. They migrated north, presumably finding more opportunity or better pay. We had our share of them.

For years the standard rate of pay was $50 per month plus board and room. No fringe benefits, no bonuses, no social security, no insurance came with it. The man came; he worked. Dad wrote him a check; he left. That was it. He may have added to our lore of stories about hired men but he didn't clutter up our records. Or the government's.

Once I remember Dad stating flatly at the dinner table that he would *never* pay a man more than $50 a month. One hired man looked at him in a rather peculiar way. But that was all.

Being a hired man, at $50 per month, was supposed to be the first step on the road to farm ownership. Hired man; then a renter; then an owner. It didn't work that way too often.

Before Geneticists Began to Play with Sex

BEFORE GENETICISTS began to play tricks on the sex life of the corn plant, getting seed for the new crop was not as simple as waiting for the salesman to convince you that a few bushels of his particular number would add 10 bushels to your yield.

In the old days you grew your own seed corn. Or rather, come early fall, you simply selected from the crop just produced some of the choicest ears to be the parents of next year's crop. It was open pollinated and in a good year produced around 50 bushels to the acre. The switch to hybrids, the major breakthrough in the agricultural revolution of the thirties and forties, shot yields up to the 75–90 bushels range, even without added fertilizer. Yet the change came slowly. Farmers had to be sold on the idea.

Before the idea was sold, or even available, Dad and I would pick our next year's seed by hand. Along in early October we would take a couple of gunnysacks, tie a loop of binder twine around one corner of the bottom and the other end around a corner of the top. You slipped the twine over your shoulder so that the sack hung down around your waist.

68

Thus armed, we started down the corn row, by that time matured and frosted. We looked for the larger ears, perhaps those pushing out through the end of their drying husks. The goal was to find the choice ear, thick, even, and filled to the tip. That was especially important you thought, little knowing that factors other than conformity were involved. As big ears were found and dropped into the sack, the load inevitably grew heavier and the binder twine cut deeper and deeper into your shoulder. So you returned to the end of the row, dumped the load, and started over again.

You also pulled a few wayward cockleburs and carried them back to the end of the field where they could be picked up and disposed of when the corn was picked up and hauled to the house.

It wasn't a big job and usually the weather was pleasant. But it was typical of the "hand operation" that marked so much of farming of the twenties and earlier.

Back at the house the carefully selected corn was pulled up beside some small outbuilding where again binder twine was called into the act. The ears were tied or looped together and hung from the rafters in strings of perhaps twenty or so. This was the drying process.

Selecting seed went on through the regular picking season too. Dad always had a small box on the side of his husking wagon and would drop an especially choice ear in that as he went along. Or he would throw ears aside as the corn was being unloaded.

Selection and drying was not the end of the process. There were the testing, shelling, and sacking, all by hand, of course.

During late winter the selected ears would be laid out in some regular order and a kernel or two selected from each ear. These kernels were then laid out on a piece of cloth perhaps 1 foot wide and 2 feet long. With a pencil, this cloth had been carefully marked out in squares so that it was possible to relate the kernel in a particular square to the ear from which it had come.

Then, beginning at one end, the cloth was tightly rolled into what was known as a "rag doll." It was tight enough so that the kernels could not become mixed or dislodged. The "doll" was tied securely, thoroughly soaked, and put in the back of the warming oven where temperatures might approximate growing conditions. After a few days or so, and continued careful watering, the "doll" was opened and the results analyzed. Most

69

of the kernels would have swelled and sprouted. But some were dormant. The parent stock of this "under-achiever" was identified and consigned to the feedlot. The proven "good guys" were put aside, eventually to have tip and butt kernels removed by hand and then put through the hand sheller to provide the final seed crop for a crop yielding about one-half or even one-third of what we expect today. The seed corn had to be "graded" too. That meant, after shelling, it was put through a hand-turned long, tin cylinder that was punctured with slots of varying sizes. Thus kernels of various sizes were segregated. So a minimum of a half-dozen nitty hand operations were involved in selecting and processing the year's seed corn.

Planting: Strictly a Job for the Expert

CORN WAS PLANTED when the oak leaves were as big as squirrels' ears. And as it is today, getting the corn planted "just right" was the single most important piece of fieldwork. Dad never entrusted *that* job to a hired man.

It was done with "Dad's team" and it was a tough job on man and horse alike. Horses sleep or rest in a standing position, frequently not lying down for long periods of time. But I can still remember Pearl and Laura, Dad's favorite team for many years, would not only lie down out in the pasture during their Sunday respite from corn planting but would stretch out as though dead. You knew they were tired.

They pulled a two-row planter, equipped with seed boxes which had a release mechanism activated by "buttons" on the planter wire.

The first step was to unroll the planter wire from one end of the field to the other. It was stretched tight and staked down at either end of the field. Every 40 inches along that wire was a "button" or a kind of big knot. The wire ran through a slotted affair on the side of the planter and each time a button came along, it moved the planter "plates" one notch and dropped two or three kernels in a hill. Click. Click. Click. Drop. Drop.

70

At the end of the field Dad swung the team around, pulled up the stake holding the wire, moved it over square behind the planter, fed the wire back into the slot on the planter, and headed back across the field. Thus, each time he crossed the field the wire was moved another few feet across the field and if the planter kept his wire evenly taut throughout the process, the corn hills could be "checked," that is, rows would be 40 inches apart and hills would be 40 inches apart in the row. Thus the field could be cultivated both ways, the way the planter went and also crossways.

And indeed corn was plowed both ways, usually twice each way before it was "laid by" about the Fourth of July when it would be knee-high. (Knee-high by the Fourth was a part of the litany of the times.)

But it was a long, slow, hard job. The seed corn had to be taken to the field. The planter boxes filled every few rounds. The wire restretched and staked at each end of the field. And if the wire jammed in the planter, which it not infrequently did, it meant long delays by going back to the end of the field, taking up the stake, repairing the wire, restretching the wire, and starting over again.

Corn planting had one other disadvantage. It could be a cold job. Early to mid-May could be cold. With many horse-drawn jobs, it was possible for the driver to get off and walk when he got cold. Not so with corn planting. He had to ride that planter and keep the team squarely on the mark. And the pressure was on. Get that corn planted. Now a farmer, in a heated cab, listening to his radio, will plant as many acres in a day as Dad could in a week—or more!

Cultivating: Every Single Hill Was Important

THE FIRST REAL FIELDWORK a young teenage farm boy would have an opportunity to do was cultivate corn. The excitement of heading out to the field the first time along with the hired men and Dad; straddling the seat of a one-row cultivator; lines tied around your back; well, it was one of those great leaps forward in the growing-up process. The corn seemed never to come up the spring that the boy was destined to take his place on the plow. Finally it was up maybe 2 or 3 inches, the soil was right, and tomorrow was the day.

The first step had been taken long before that. That was to find, out in the grove, a branch maybe 4 feet long with a neat fork in the end. This was trimmed down so that the forked ends were only 2 or 3 inches long.

The day arrived. The team (yours was the oldest, safest) was hitched to a one-row cultivator, the forked stick carefully lodged up in the frame, the lines knotted to go around the driver's back so that both hands were free. You started, ever so slowly, down that first row of small corn, little sensing it was the beginning of a routine that would in due course become as deadly as herding cows on the road.

There was much adjusting of the shovels. Dad came by to check. The shields, which kept the dirt from covering the young shoots, needed careful attention. But in spite of all care, a hill of corn would be covered up. Whereupon the team was stopped and the forked stick was brought into action; boy, hired man, and Dad, all, would lean back and carefully uncover that hill with its two or three corn plants.

Farming was that kind of business. Each hill of corn was important to the point of stopping the whole procedure to un-cover it—by hand. When harvest came the ears on those stalks would be picked, one at a time—by hand. Taken into the crib, it might even be scooped off the wagon—by hand. Eventually it would be shelled. Much of it would be pushed into the sheller—by hand. It would be elevated, in the shelled state, into a wagon. And then if it was being used for feed it would be scooped into the feed wagon or bunk—by hand. Cobs would pile up on one side of the sheller. They would be scooped into a wagon, taken either to the cob house or shoved into a basement window—by hand. Eventually, a pail at a time, they would end up in the kitchen cookstove. Finally, the ashes would be carried out—by hand. The energy cycle was complete.

When the corn was small plowing went as slow as a team would walk. The slower the better to keep from covering the corn and still move just the right amount of soil up around each hill and row, thus covering weeds that weren't plowed out.

72

The second time over, "crossing the corn," the team would be pushed along more rapidly. But we had many rows a half mile long and you would make mighty few rounds in half a day.

Birds, ground squirrels, and an occasional snake were around. Or a mother pheasant and her brood. Sometimes a car came along the nearby road or a freight train over on the other side of the fields. Usually you cultivated in a field with a hired man or two. But you each had your own "land," maybe two dozen rows each was working on, a row at a time. So you did not pass close as the two or three teams crossed and re-crossed the fields, stopping, uncovering corn, pulling cockleburs while your horses rested, checking the manes under their collars.

It was quiet. The horses switched flies. The tugs jingled a little. The harness creaked. The soft dirt rolled up on the wheels and, if there was a breeze, blew it in your shoes and maybe all over you if the breeze was strong enough. Would noon never come? Or 6 o'clock?

The excitement of that first day paled as cultivating continued, day after day, from the time school was out until "laying by" time came.

When the corn was near the laying by stage, it was large enough to brush gently against your overalls as you continued to straddle the row and guide the shovels down the row. Early morning would find those corn plants loaded with heavy dew. Before you had half crossed the field the inside of your pants, clear to your crotch, would be soaking wet. By midmorning you would be pretty well dried out.

Everyone has experienced the awfulness of trying to stay awake in a meeting, in church, or in some public place. That experience was never more painful than in the total privacy of a cornfield.

It was after dinner. The temperature was near 90. The humidity was high. On all sides was greenness, shimmering in the heat, knee-high or better. The corn plants seemed to suck up the heat and throw it back at the boy on the cultivator. The horses plodded down those endless rows . . . plod, plod, plod. The wheels and the shovels made a soft "soil sound" as you moved quietly along. You were bent over, watching for that next corn plant—and they came on endlessly one after another. It was awful. You vowed, when the cause was having been up too late the night before, that you would be in bed with the chickens, or

73

else. By evening, of course, that was forgotten—sufficiently at least to prevent any interference with nocturnal plans.

Of course, the counter situation was to be caught at the far side of a half-mile field in a sudden, cold rain with at most no more than a jacket. You were totally drenched, water squishing in your shoes, by the time you reached the house. And before *you* dried off, the team had to be unhitched and put in the barn.

Cultivating was not all bad. You learned to know every foot of soil in a field, where every patch of weeds was, where the pocket gophers worked, and to marvel at the growth of corn from one time over to the next. You felt as though you almost knew each plant individually.

And, of course, so much of the family welfare was tied directly to the progress of those fields of corn that only the most insensitive could avoid some sense of excitement as that remarkable crop developed so rapidly. You were a part of the process.

This kind of farming was long, long before the days of herbicides, of course. Mechanical means—pulling, hoeing, cultivating—were used to discourage the weeds.

Morning glories were among the worst. I can remember too well starting into a patch of glories with a corn plow and shortly they would have balled up in front of the cultivator to the point you could go no farther. You backed the team slightly and got down and clawed out the mass of weeds and dirt which had ganged up in front of the plow. You were careful to throw the weeds over onto the rows you had cultivated; otherwise they were there to stall your operation on the return trip.

Morning glories were not the worst weed but they were pretty bad. They matted together in big patches, one vine joining another and so on.

We had a neighbor with a quaint sense of humor. He had a field that was particularly infested. Someone asked him if it didn't seem unusually bad. "Sure is," he responded, "You can pick up one corner and shake the whole darned field."

74

Poets and Painters Never Set Up a Shock

NEXT TO SLEIGHING off to Grandmother's house for Christmas dinner, probably more artists and more poets have used shocks of small grain and corn—particularly corn—to create illusions of the goodness of the good old days than any other object of the countryside. Overlooked in these quaint calendar scenes is the fact that these two harvest views represented some of the hardest and most disagreeable work at a time and place when there was plenty of that; not the hardest, but among the hardest.

75

Take those small-grain shocks, for instance. The horse- or later the tractor-drawn binder would kick off these bundles of freshly cut oats, barley, or wheat as it circled the field. Small grain was cut at a greener stage then than it is now cut by combine. And weeds would be bound into the bundle. I make the point that the bundles were heavy. But they had to be put in shocks where they would remain "curing" for a couple of weeks until it was time to thresh.

So down each row would go a couple of men and maybe a middle-sized boy. Bundles were picked up, one under each arm, and set down together, leaning on each other. Normally they would stand in that position until two more were picked up and put on one side of the original two. Then the same on the other end. Then two might be put on either side of the original two, making a kind of egg-shaped shock out of either six or eight bundles. Then a bundle was flattened out, both head and butt, and placed lengthwise as a cap on the shock. By noon, or night, leaning over, picking them up, setting them down—with the temperature in the high 80s or 90s at harvesttime—turned into just a plain miserable day's work. The burlap-covered water jug never looked so good as when you made it back to the end of the field where it was hidden under a shock. Of course once in a while the knotter on the binder would miss a beat and you would find a pile of loose grain. Granddad Heaton, who had followed the old cradles before the day of the McCormick reaper, could grab a handful of straw and with a couple of quick twists bind up a bundle as tight as it would have come from the binder.

But that was not all. After a windstorm, some shocks always had to be rebuilt or at least recapped. Possibly if it had rained heavily about the time the threshing machine was due at your place, it would be desirable to go out and push all the shocks over so they would have a chance to dry out. It was for certain of these reasons, quite aside from the threshing process, that combines were developed.

Later in the fall, usually after school had started fortunately, it was time to make corn fodder. Here again the horse-drawn binder took off across the field and left at regular intervals bundles of fodder—stalk, ear and all—cut off about 6 inches above

76

the ground. There were probably two dozen stalks in a bundle. Corn for fodder was cut well before it was dry and ripe, and thus was green and heavy. Here it was necessary to start building the shock around a "horse." The horse was a pole 10 or 12 feet long made out of a sapling with a couple of legs about 4 feet long attached to the larger end. The horse would be set where the shock was to be built and you lugged bundles up and leaned them against the horse. Eventually, as the bundles leaned against each other, the shock took on some stability. The horse was pulled out and the shock finished with perhaps fifteen or so bundles. Each shock was tied with binder twine. A day of that activity was the kind that made it difficult to get hired men.

That was not the end. Sometime in the winter that shock had to be brought into the feedyard. Before I went to school in the morning, Dad and I would hitch up and head out to the fodder field with a hayrack. The rack, bouncing over the ridges of frozen ground, would rattle and tilt off at crazy angles; it was nothing more than a kind of basket arrangement about 8 feet wide and 12 or so feet long.

I would drive the team and load the fodder. Dad would pitch on the bundles. By then many were frozen down and had to be cut loose. The last bundle up on the rack would send field mice scurrying in all directions. It seemed the wind was always blowing. The bundles were stiff and sometimes full of snow and ice. The idea of loading them was to place them in neat and orderly rows, one on top of the other, and build them up as high as Dad could pitch them, which with a fork would be 10 feet or so. If they were frozen, which they always were, and the wind was blowing, which it seemed always to do, the load would likely develop great bulges and lumps and unevenness and bundles would slip off the back of the rack, or worse yet, right back down on the same side from which Dad had just pitched them up. Even then it wasn't until the load was supposedly on that the real trial began. The field, frozen and uneven, was especially so if it were necessary to drive crossways of the field, opposite to the way the corn was plowed over the last time. The rack, with its bulky load catching all the wind that was going, developed great unseaworthiness. The worst that could happen was to upset the whole thing. Dad and I, rack, and all would turn over in a shower of frozen cornstalks and snow. Or perhaps just a big

77

piece of the load would slip off one side. In either case we had only one solution: stop and load up.

No artist painting those quaint shocks ever had to throw a load on the hayrack and take it to the feedyard.

Of All the Drudgery, Corn Picking the Worst

SHOCKING OATS and corn fodder were tough jobs, but they didn't hold the proverbial candle to corn picking. In the first place it was harder work; it was the nearest thing to drudgery on farms before the day of mechanical pickers. It *was* drudgery. And it went on and on through weeks and weeks and weeks of back-breaking work that began at the first streak of light, went on until dark and through the cold, late, fall rains, the early snows, and frequently after the ground was frozen. Imagine, if you can, picking by hand every single ear of corn that you see in some of the cribs or in the great piles of corn you admire as you drive so casually out across the fall countryside.

Here's the way it went:

A wagon was rigged up with a set of bangboards on one side. On the low side the box would be 36 inches high, a standard wagon box. On the far side, or the right side, the box was built up perhaps another 4 or 5 feet with the bangboards. Next a supply of perhaps a dozen pairs of double-thumbed, cotton-flannel husking gloves was laid in. Double-thumbed so you could turn them over when one thumb wore out and a dozen pairs because you would wear out both sides of a good many gloves in the season. Why? Because the ears themselves were rough and by the time the corn was dry enough to pick, the leaves and stalks were a standing plant of sharp, serrated edges which tore up gloves, wore out jackets and overalls, and left exposed wrists raw and even bleeding. The pickers would use great quantities of livestock salve on wrists and hands each noon and night to keep their hands from cracking and bleeding. Added to that discomfort was the fact that picking always began before the frost dried off in the morning. If there was snow or rain gloves could be a soggy mess.

78

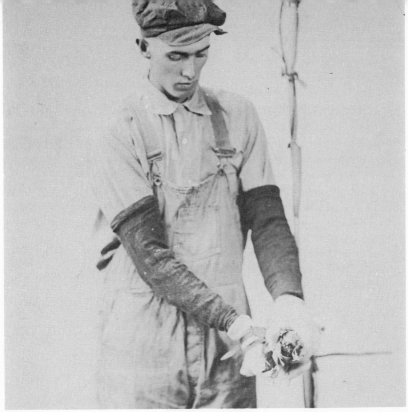

The first step in the corn-picking process. Old cotton stockings, worn for added protection over wrists and arms, were typical; Dad always wore them.

The next item was the husking peg or hook. Either one was a metal gadget strapped across the palm of the right hand. Raised out of the center of the metal, and directly in the palm of the hand, was a hook perhaps a half inch high and as wide.

In operation, the husker grabbed the ear of corn in the left hand while with the right hand he quickly raked the hook across the husks, pulling them away from one side of the ear. With the left hand he pulled them off the other side, snapped the ear off at the shank, and heaved it without looking at the bangboard where it hit and fell into the wagon. Before one ear hit another was on the way and the picker was eyeing the next. He worked methodically back and forth on two rows, while he giddaped his team to take a few steps and keep abreast of him as he picked

79

along or said a "whoa now" when the wagon got too far ahead. The team soon learned.

By midfall not all the stalks would still be standing. A windstorm might have not only put many ears on the ground but laid stalks over until it was a matter not only of picking but of stepping over, leaning down then to ground level, and then pushing aside stalks in the path of progress.

This process began at daylight. We had a neighbor who went to the field with a lantern and waited until it was light enough to see the corn. It went on at a dead heat pace until noon. By then a good picker would have filled his wagon and moved some of the bangboards from the high side over to the near side. If he was really good, his load would be 50 inches deep, representing 50 bushels of ear corn and he was on his way to a 100-bushel day which was the goal of many. Then it was into the buildings with a creaking load, unload it, have a quick dinner, and go back to repeat that process until dark.

(To visualize, even remotely, this task, try to think of the kind of day you would put in if you simply had the task of throwing into a wagon box—an ear at a time—from a pile of corn *already picked* the equivalent of nearly 100 bushels a day. You did it in rain and occasional snow, in heat and cold as it might come. And before you started in the morning you got up in time to feed and curry and hitch your team and stayed at the assignment late enough at night to do those same chores after dark.)

At dark the wagons would come back out of the fields, loaded, pulling heavy, with the weary picker seated atop a bulging load which he would even out before he started for the house to keep ears from falling to the ground. If it had rained, or the ground was soft, the wheels would be caked with mud and foxtail and the team would be puffing by the time it reached the house. There the wagons would line up, the first man pulling his load into the hoist and taking his team to put on the power. "The power" was a geared arrangement to which was attached a sweep extending out perhaps 14 feet. The team was hitched to this sweep and the inside horse "tied in" so that the team, when it started, moved in a circle. A "tumbling rod" transmitted the power from this arrangement to the elevator and a hoist which raised the front end of the wagon.

The team started. The elevator began to move its endless chain, the hoist began to howl as the front end of the wagon

80

*If your back hurts looking at this picture, bear in mind
this man will pick two wagonloads of corn a day, stooping
over to pick up many down ears and tossing them all,
one at a time, into the wagon.*

swung clear of the ground and the picker pulled out the lower
board on his endgate, leaving an opening 12 inches deep and 36
inches wide. The corn picker got down on his knees and regu-
lated the flow of corn out of the upended box (tilted about 45
degrees) so that it fed in a steady stream onto the elevator.

Assuming all went well, the elevator chain did not break,
and it was not necessary to go up into the crib to unplug a spout,
the load might be off in 15 minutes. It was time to move that
wagon out, pull the next in, drop the tugs but leave the team
standing, and begin the process all over again.

It was dark and even on those few farms with electricity, it was long before the time of the present-day fluorescent type which lights the whole barnyard. Instead the whole process was carried on in semidarkness and it was totally dark by the time the horses were in the barn, unharnessed, fed, and the men, dog tired, were on the way to the house for supper. Before daylight the next morning they would begin the process all over again.

Of course, some rains and snows stopped the picking. Mother dreaded those times particularly, anticipating, as she put it, "a bunch of corn pickers loafing around the house." And that's exactly what it was. Regular hired men, paid by the month, would live with the family as one of the family. And always there were fences to be fixed, buildings to be repaired, barns to be cleaned out, stock to be cared for regardless of the weather. But corn pickers were hired to pick corn by the bushel, room and board furnished. If they couldn't pick they didn't work. But they did eat. And they did loaf around the house. And while they might be good corn pickers (and then again they might not; you took what you could get), they were not always the kind of

fellows you would invite in for Sunday dinner. To end up having them as "house guests" for a few days of nasty weather was not appreciated. Remember, there was no television or radio to help relieve the tensions or the monotony.

Sprained wrists were not unusual during corn picking time and many pickers kept their wrists wrapped, or wore tightly laced or buckled leather gauntlets or wrist bindings. Corn picking was a test of man against the elements, of stamina, and it was this fact that led to the drama of early corn picking contests, county, state, and national. These drew great crowds of people, such was the admiration for the husky young farm lad who could stand out in such competition. The pickers in these contests, of course, went in for short bursts of time, not the all-day, daylight-to-dark, grind. The contestants would line up at the end of the field, some stripped to the waist (to hell with the harshness of those frozen cornstalks) and launch into a frenzy of picking for perhaps 40 minutes at the sound of the starter's gun. It wasn't the size of the load only but also how many ears were left in the field and how many "ribbons" (shucks) were left on the ears in their wagon.

Corn picking by hand was among the hardest of farm jobs. But fame went to the brawny young farmer who took top honors in the national corn picking contests that attracted many, many thousands.

83

If this process seems descriptive of an era which no one wishes to recapture, bear in mind the period before elevators became common. That was even less inviting. The load, picked an ear at a time, was pulled up alongside the crib and the whole rear of the wagon was opened by letting down a "scoop board." The picker then completed his day's labors by scooping the load off—throwing it over the side of the wagon, over the side of the crib, and frequently higher than his head. He didn't need to study the manual of air force exercises after that operation.

The Threshing Ring: A Community Effort

IT WAS ALWAYS the "threshing ring"; never a group or a co-op or anything like that. A dozen or more farm families, usually on adjoining farms, made up the "community" for this particular effort. Exchanging work with the close neighbors for haying, corn shelling, butchering, and castrating the pigs was always done a lot. But threshing was a big community effort. It took a big machine and a good-sized engine of some kind. Usually this was owned outright by one farmer and he received custom payment for the use of the equipment which he personally managed.

Everything else was worked out cooperatively. The larger farmer would be expected to furnish two men, perhaps himself with a team and wagon and a hired man who would pitch bundles. The men who pitched bundles in the field were called "spike pitchers." The bundle hauler would drive up and down the rows of shocks and throw on enough bundles to load the bed of his rack. Then he would climb aboard and a spike pitcher would come by and toss on the rest of the bundles while the driver loaded them.

Six or eight teams and racks might be loading in the field at one time. Loaded they would head for the house, wait their turn to pitch their bundles into the machine, and then go back for another load.

Others would be responsible for taking the grain to a granary in a barn or crib. Oats were fed, mostly to horses, seldom sold.

84

Because this operation considerably enlarged the normal community, threshing time always brought news, some gossip, and maybe some new ideas. Each farmer would see a farm operation and be in a farm home that he would not otherwise have an opportunity to visit. So when Dad would return at night he usually had some comment about the day's activities that added interest to the supper table. Supper was late because they would work until 6 or so and then, depending upon where they were threshing, the men would have to drive their teams and racks 2 or 3 miles to get home. But they often started late in the morning, 9 or so, because the dew would make the grain too "tough" to thresh.

Threshing would last for about two weeks, depending upon weather and size of the run. Completion of the operation marked a definite dividing point in summer activity. It was the first "break" since oat seeding started in late March or early April. Hence at the last job on the run there was always a bit of a "school's out" atmosphere. At some places everyone threw his old straw hat in the threshing machine as he finished unloading his last load. At Moneta we lived in a German community where they enjoyed their schnapps. One year our place was the last job. It was cider-making time. But lacking refrigeration the juice got a little "high." So did the threshers. The cider, the straw hats, and the job all finished up together.

Dad shook his head. Such tomfoolery was not his way of doing business.

Dinner for Twenty

FOR THE FARM WIFE the romance of threshing was a little on the dubious side. Neighbors' wives came in to help, exchanging work in the kitchens just as their husbands did out in the field. Usually two or three would show up shortly after breakfast to begin peeling potatoes, setting the table, and all the rest. Not many homes were fixed for twenty people to sit down to eat at one time; so not infrequently some planks would be set up along some improvised tables, even out in the yard.

COURTESY ISU HISTORY COLLECTION

*The old-fashioned threshing dinner has been much
romanticized but not by the farm wife confronted with
feeding 20 or 25 ravenous men without the aid of
refrigeration, frozen foods, running water, or any heat
but the old kitchen stove.*

Mother recalls in particular the threshing dinners she fixed
as a bride out on the old Hamilton farm. With horse and buggy
they went to town the night before to get the meat. It was always beef. Then the meal was prepared on the old kitchen range
and the men were fed in the kitchen. It took some doing, Mother
remembers, simply to work out the logistics of cooking, serving,
and seating all in the same room, even though it was a large
kitchen. On top of everything else, the kitchen was unbearably
hot with the heat of the stove which had been going full blast for
half a day.

Several pails of warm water always had to be on hand at the
back gate, along with soap, wash pans, and towels hanging over
the fence. And of course it wasn't that you knew for certain the
crew would be there at any given time. Maybe you were all fired
up and it began raining at 10 o'clock. Everyone would go home
with mountains of mashed potatoes in the works. Or, worse yet,

86

maybe they happened to finish up at the neighbor's 2 hours early and the first bundle wagons started down the road for your place at 10:30 or so. Naturally, there was some give-and-take among the wives under such circumstances; but things would get a little tense nevertheless.

Whether they liked to admit it or not, a certain degree of competition existed among the wives. One of the first questions when Dad came home at night was: "What did Mrs. Jensen have for dinner?"

Mother, assuring herself and the family that "it is about as cheap as anything," served fried chicken and ice cream more than once. That menu was not soon topped.

The many myths about threshing all include the old threshing ring, and threshers sitting down to dinner (as seen by Grant Wood), a lot of neighborliness and camaraderie, and all that sort of thing. What they forget, and it's just as well, is the dirt, the dust, the heat, and the hard work. Especially the dirt and dust.

Before Dad and Mother left the farm, and before the revolution in farm machinery put the old threshing ring out of business, it became not uncommon to take the crew to town for dinner. Heavens, what was the world coming to? Well, it was changing.

Eating Dust for the Sake of a Strawstack

SINCE WE HAD lots of livestock around our place, we had a great need to save all the straw for bedding, for feed, and for winter protection around the strawstack.

The threshing machine was known officially as a separator for that is exactly what it did, separate the oats from the straw. Typically the machine would dispose of the straw by aiming its big blower out in one direction and the straw would build up in a huge irregular mound of haphazard proportions. But that was wasteful and the sign of a poor farmer. The alternative was to set the blower on an automatic gear which caused it to move back and forth in a kind of half-moon effect. Then a farmer like

Dad would put his shirt on the outside of his overalls, button up his collar, put a handkerchief around his neck, take a pitchfork, and begin to build a stack. As the straw was blown out on the ground, Dad would carefully push the output into an outline of the stack he wanted to build, perhaps 20 feet wide at the base and 60 or 70 feet in semicircular length.

The blower moved automatically from one end of the stack to the other, followed methodically by Dad, waist deep in the loose straw, carefully building his stack. The only problem was that the full blast from the blower hit the stack builder full force each time the blower came by, each round that it made. He could not escape. There was nothing to do but shut his eyes, turn his back, and have the full blast of oats straw, chaff, dust, and dirt blown into every crack and crevice of his clothes while he inhaled it with each breath.

The only thing worse than building such a stack, which might take a day of such labor, was blowing the straw into the barn. There again it was button up all crevices and, before the days of inhalators and masks, go into the haymow where he had no opportunity to breathe anything but pure dust and oats straw and chaff. It was like miner's "black lung." Dad would cough and spit oats dust for days afterward and his eyes would be fiery red. Grant Wood never captured that part of threshing.

But Dad was so proud of his nice symmetrical strawstacks that as soon as threshing was over, he would carefully clean up around the base of the stack, saving the "crumbs" from his careful sculpture, and fence the stack so the cattle would not eat it before winter.

The Steam Engine's Demise: End of an Era

AT CERTAIN TIMES now in the midsummer season it is not difficult to see an old steam engine and threshing machine at work—recreated for the sake of nostalgia and usually for a fee at the gate!

I didn't realize it at the time, but the transition from that era to combustion engines once took place right on our place in

*In a few isolated instances the old steam-powered
threshing machine held on into the forties. But most
were in junkyards before that time and in the scrap
drives went to World War II.*

the midst of threshing. It was in the early twenties and a steamer
was providing the power for our threshing ring up in Clay
County.

An old steamer *was* exciting, particularly for kids. When the
rig was at our place, Dad would get up earlier than usual and go
out and light the fire under the boiler so that it would have a
head of steam up in time to start work. The water wagon and the
coal cart were parked nearby.

A boy of today could hold no more respect for a pilot of a

89

COURTESY *Wallaces Farmer*

*As the old steam engines went out of business, they were
replaced with such monster internal combustion machines
as the Rumley Oil Pull, used for threshing, silo filling,
and occasionally even for plowing.*

jumbo jet than I held for that engineer who, always with a red
handkerchief around his neck, mounted the steps of that mam-
moth machine and began to push and pull the levers that activated either the flywheel for the belt or the slow movement of that
ponderous machine itself.

It was so quiet it was almost frightening. All that power and
no sound. Just the gentlest, quietest little putt-putt, a kind of a
gasp, and those great wheels began to roll. Or the flywheel began
to turn over ever so slowly and the belt, twisted and swaying
lightly in the breeze, began to transmit the power of the engine
to the separator 75 feet away. The whole complicated machine
came slowly alive. Belts, some twisted, some straight on, laced
either side of the machine. Slowly they began to move and jiggle,
rotate, or in other ways implement all the complicated mechanism it took to separate the grain from the straw. Men stood on
either side, watching as it gathered speed, alert to belts jumping
off or other problems.

At the front end, where the bundles would soon be starting
through for separating, a series of arms, each mounted with ser-

90

rated teeth, began to reach out and claw the air, their ultimate purpose being to pull the grain into the machine for separating.

There had been talk that the old steamer "might not last another season." It didn't. Something vital gave way while the job was in process at our place. No doubt it was a financial blow to someone.

Since something had to be done an internal combustion tractor, a Hart-Parr from, I believe, Charles City, was on the job in a few days. What noise, compared to the steamer! The new tractor pulled the old steamer out into our grove where it stayed for some time (to the great satisfaction of all neighborhood boys). Finally the junk man from Spencer came and claimed it for recycling.

Much of the romance, the little there was, went out of threshing at that moment. Little did we realize that the next step would be to do away with the whole process. In two more decades (more or less) each farmer was buying his own combine and one of the things that held neighborhoods and communities together, the old threshing ring, was no more.

Haymaking: Just a Forkful at a Time

A MOWER with a 5-foot bar of serrated teeth would seem to have been a fairly dangerous piece of equipment for a kid, but there was a lot of boy work in haymaking. The team knew as much or more than the boy did so everything went well.

The first cutting was in the pleasant part of June. With a great sense of accomplishment you went round and round the field, watching the standing hay falling in neat rows—round after round—and giving off an aroma the like of which there is no other. Meadowlarks, rabbits, and maybe pheasants abounded. The hayfield had been their refuge and you felt badly as you brought about its destruction, especially as you came to a nest, particularly a pheasant nest. When that occurred I would always try to lift the cycle bar and jump over the nest, but it was not a very successful operation. Left was only a little patch of standing hay and by the time the field was raked and loaded onto the racks, the old hen had been frightened completely away and the nest was deserted.

Given twenty-four hours of good drying weather, the next operation was raking, another boy job. Again the same quiet team on a hay rake of the old-fashioned kind which literally combed the field. As the rake filled up, you would kick the trip and the load would dump. The idea was to dump each load so that finally the whole field was a series of rows reaching from one side of the field to the other.

The curing process went on briefly with the hay in the wind-rows. The length of curing time depended upon drying conditions—temperature, humidity, wind.

All this time, of course, you are scanning the skies and hoping for perhaps three days of sunshine. After maybe only a half day, the boy was back in the field and the raking process went crossways of the field, straddling the windrows and leaving the hay in bunches or "cocks" as they were sometimes called.

By then, weather cooperating, it was time for Dad and the hired man or the neighbors to join the effort.

We would head for the field with the hayracks and pitchforks. I would drive the team, following the row of cocks across the field, stopping by each one while one man pitched the hay onto the rack so that it gradually built up into a square, even load maybe 10 feet high from ground to top of load. Thus the man on the ground was pitching heavy forkfuls of hay as high over his head as he could reach, on and on and on. No need for any special arm, back, or shoulder exercises for that man on the ground. The job was traded off and gradually the boy on the rack grew up enough to handle the loading process, although that was not as simple as it seemed, for awkward loading would let a whole corner of a load fall off as the wagon rocked along on the way to the barn. This met with Dad's keen displeasure.

Once loaded, all hands climbed on top of the load, sank down in the soft hay, clucked to the team which seemed far below, and headed for the barn. It was a pleasant interlude. The oats were ripening to gold. The corn was solid green. The smell of hay was sweet. The June sky was unblemished blue as far as the eye could see. It was beautiful.

The rack swayed gently from side to side and one drove carefully to keep it balanced. Careful driving was called for at

Hoisting a forkful of hay into the haymow. Driving the team on the fork was a boy's job (or sometimes a woman's).

the barn where the haymow door had been opened, leaving a great cavernous opening up at the very peak of the building. The load must center directly under that opening. The boy then hitched his team to the hay rope attached to the hayfork. This big, fierce-looking piece of equipment, an upside-down, U-shaped item perhaps 3 feet high, was sharp enough so it could be driven deep into the load of loose hay. It was then "set" by pulling a smaller rope attached to a mechanism that caused some small levers to expand out into the hay at the tip of the fork—a kind of a fishhook effect. The fork was attached to one end of the hay rope which ran up to the peak of the open haymow door, the full length of the barn, down the back of the barn, and up to the

93

front of the barn. Here waited the boy and his team. Ever so slowly, the team began to put tension on the rope.

It pulled and creaked through pulleys as it ran twice the length of the barn and down into the fork.

The boy with the team kept a wary eye on the operation, ready for a sudden stop in case of emergency. Slowly a forkful of hay would start toward the gaping haymow door in the scene that has been romanticized by Grant Wood and many others. At the peak of the barn, the fork locked into the track and began to move back into the barn where Dad, "mowing the hay away" would shout "whoa!" This was the signal for the team to stop and the man on the rack to pull the trip rope dropping the hay into the mow. There, much harder (and frequently very hot) work was going on in pushing the hay back out to the side of the mow.

It took perhaps six or eight such operations to clear a rackful of hay. Then it was back to the field to start over.

Now farmers put up very little hay. It is easy to see why. What they do put up is by procedures not even remotely related to the good old days. And that is a good thing, although some parts of the operation were pleasing, particularly for a boy; he didn't have to pitch the loads or work in the mow.

On some farms, I am reminded by my mother and sister, women often drove the team on the fork; but not on ours.

Burning Stalks: Pretty, But Not Good

IT WASN'T GOOD AGRONOMY. But it was necessary and it was pretty at night.

The first operation in getting ready to plant corn in the spring was to "break the stalks." This was an early April job, in the first warm days after the oats were seeded. The job meant taking a spiked tooth harrow or drag (the likes of which are still used) and dragging the field of old cornstalks. This broke them loose from the roots and then the field was raked with the old-fashioned hay rake, the kind you see now only in machinery museums or in pictures. Essentially you "combed" the whole

94

Raking stalks in the springtime prior to burning them:
a practice that lent beauty to the countryside but was
poor agronomy.

field and by dumping the rake at regular intervals, created long rows of cornstalks maybe 2 or 3 feet high. By the time I got home from school, Dad or the hired man would have fields of stalks raked into long rows ready to be burned.

It was a great job for a boy—fascinating. You lit one end of the long row, the end upwind. Then the trick was to get a stalk with the shucks still intact, hold it in the blaze until it was burning well and then race to the next row, 30 or 40 feet away. That was your torch. The game was to see how few matches you could use.

Shortly you would look back from the far corner of the field and see fires moving steadily from one side to the other, a layer of smoke hanging over it all and drifting off across the countryside—therapy for the arsonist.

Of course, some of the fire lines would have breaks so the field had to be watched and gone over again. If it were dry or too windy there was always danger of the fire getting into the fence row and burning off the fence posts. This could be frightening; a fire out of control would bring Dad on the run and with

95

our jackets and feet we would try to beat and stamp out the flames.

These fires would burn into the evening, and across the countryside one could see stalk fires burning on all sides. It was pretty. The smell of spring was in the air; another year was beginning.

But weren't farmers burning up humus that should have been plowed under? Yes, of course. So why did they do it? In the first place, the concern for the soil was still a good many years away. After all, a few patches of original prairie were still to be tiled and put to corn.

But an even more important reason for burning the stalks was the fact that the horsepower and equipment were simply not sufficient for the task of cutting up and incorporating much heavy forage in the soil. It was difficult enough to get the seedbed worked down and ready for planting without the handicap of a layer of old cornstalks. So they were burned. And it was pretty at night.

Herding Cows: A "Man-killing" Boy's Job

"A BOY'S JOB that kills off a man." That was the common and abundantly deserved description of grazing cows on the road, a practice now virtually unknown. Where it does exist, technology has again taken over. A strand of electric fence replaces the yawning boy and his pony.

But imagine this situation: a delightful summer day, maybe a little hot but not unpleasant. Corn maybe 6 inches to fence high; the oats ripening.

The country road, a strip of dirt about one car-width wide. In a half day perhaps a half-dozen cars tool along at 30 miles an hour, one of them the mailman. The others are all neighbors. The loudest sound is a cow nipping off a mouthful of bluegrass or belching it up for further chewing.

The horse, held by rein or a long rope, grazes nearby, his bridle rattling as he chases flies from an exposed flank. The sad-

96

dle creaks; the stirrups rattle. A meadowlark whose nest is threatened by a grazing calf expresses frustration or if it is unmolested gives forth with a trill of melody. The bumblebees hover over the wild roses and you give them a fair berth. Ground squirrels talk back and forth and scurry across the road as the cows move leisurely from place to place. The skies are clear and blue and the idea there could ever be enough smoke in the world to darken them is beyond comprehension. The dust storms are still to come and the word *pollution* is unknown.

It was a picture of bucolic contentment—unless the cows were unusually restless and tended to wander too far. The boy found himself a comfortable spot along the roadbank, or against the fence row, smoothed down the grass and settled down with the latest issue of *The American Boy*. What more could you want?

Little did you realize how much you would long for a small slice of that experience to drop in at regular intervals in the hurry-hurry, helter-skelter that was to be your pace in times to come. For the job was an overwhelming bore. Grown men so hated it they assigned the task to boys too small to rebel or resist. Those were the longest hours of a boy's life, frequently put in without the aid of a timepiece. For this was long before every youngster carried a watch. You gauged the time by the sun, or the mailman, or the cream truck, or when the men in the field started toward the house at noontime.

Sometimes the cows hated it too. If the flies got too bad or the day was too hot and the cows wanted water, the whole herd would take off on a dead run for home. Presumably the boy would try to head them off and keep them grazing, but his heart wasn't in the assignment. The cows always won and Dad, working in the nearby field, was obviously aware that something less than a superlative effort had gone into the resistance effort.

The worst thing that could happen to a cow herder was to have the cows, either as you daydreamed or even as you were alertly on the job, break over into the lushness of the neighbor's cornfield. You were panic-stricken. The cows would push through a hole in the fence and race off in all directions, devouring great mouthfuls of the tender young corn plants. They would nip small plants off at ground level or pull them roots and all; higher plants would break off as the cows rushed up the rows. You were responsible for this devastation taking place before

97

your eyes and would be held accountable. The worst of all situations prevailed if the field happened to belong to a neighbor whose friendship was something less than complete. That was when the word *confrontation* developed, when you tried to explain to your father how anything like that could happen when all in the world you had to do, ah yes, all in the world, was *watch those cows.*

Why did you herd cows on the road? It was because you were poor and help (the small-boy variety) was cheap. If you could supplement your pasture with a few acres of roadside grazing, well, that's what you did. There was always too little pasture because pasture didn't pay like corn and oats and although grain prices grew progressively lower, the acres constantly increased in a treadmill sort of effort to "keep up."

Driving Cattle Out of the River Pasture

WHEN WE FARMED near Glidden the acres were put to corn and oats and during that time our herd of Angus was taken to a river pasture on the old Hamilton farm, 10 miles northeast of Glidden.

As soon as the pasture was adequate in the spring, Dad and I, with perhaps two dozen cows and calves and sometimes a horse we would take turns riding, would head for the river pasture. No cattle trucks were to be had and if there had been we wouldn't have hired them; that would have cost money.

It was a good day's work: driving the cows, turning them at the right corners, keeping them from turning in at farmyards where they wouldn't be welcome, and out of fields that might not be adequately fenced. It was slow going, often hot. We never carried water but expected to get a drink at farm pumps along the way. My thirst was unquenchable. I could barely last from one pump to another yet Dad—I thought he must be some kind of camel—could and would go for miles between drinks. It was a long, slow drag for a boy.

I am sure the countryside was beautiful—spring, birds, flowers coming into bloom. Everything the poet writes about. I

98

didn't see a single one of those things; they were so commonplace. I was tired and thirsty; so thirsty.

Late in the afternoon we would turn the cows and calves into the river pasture, unsaddle the horse, and leave him there too until the return trip in the fall. Someone would come in a car and take us back home, a merciful trip!

On Sundays during the summer we would go out to "salt the cattle." Originally we bought cattle salt by the barrel. We would take out a pailful of loose salt on Sunday and the cattle would come quickly as it was poured out in little mounds. Later it was block salt in blocks about a foot square. These were occasions, too, to check up on the cattle—count them, note their condition, and check any signs of ill health.

Going to the Sandhills for Feeder Cattle

In ADDITION to the herd of purebred Angus which were Dad's pride and joy, we nearly always, as the saying went, "had something in the feedlot." A couple of years it was upward of a thousand lambs. But usually it was cattle; good cattle. Frequently we had the opportunity to make more money feeding "plain" or "ordinary" cattle which meant they were crossbreeds, including some dairy blood, long-legged, thin-faced, unattractive. But Dad always got so much satisfaction just out of fattening "good cattle" that that was the kind we always fed. Usually calves, weighing 400–500 pounds in the fall, went to market the next summer at 1,000 pounds: Good to Choice.

One year, a year that I think was a financial disaster, Dad and Uncle Clyde bought several carloads of calves out in the sandhills of Cherry County, Nebraska. The town was Wood Lake. I had never been west of Omaha. That little cow town of Wood Lake, dropped down in those rolling hills of Cherry County where we could drive for miles between ranch houses, was a fascination to me. We stayed at a typical little unmodern hotel where the cowboys tied their horses at the hitching rack at the sidewalk and swaggered into the hotel, complete with boots, spurs, and big hats. The cowboys would be bringing in large droves of calves and yearlings, herds that would string out for a half mile as they came in over the hills and into yards. Once yarded the owner would quickly put a stout chain around the gate and secure it with a padlock.

This wasn't to thwart the rustlers, as I first thought. When the first locomotive came chugging up by those yards, those cattle would turn into wild beasties. They would make a run for the far side of the yard, pile up, jump on each other's backs and the timbers and planks and posts would strain and creak and give. It took a lot to hold them.

We bought our cattle from the Tethrow Ranch and it was heady stuff for a Corn Belt raised boy, even one raised on a horse, to see my counterparts jump on a not very well-trained bronco and head miles off to the other side of the ranch to round up cattle, past windmills and watering holes and ponds, some with a fair number of ducks.

The wind blew all the time. In town, where grass cover had been long gone, the sand blew all the time. And out on the ranch wherever a trail or a road would cut through the prairie, the sand would blow away and there would be a "blow out." If this happened in a trail or a road they wanted to keep in use they patched the blow out with a layer of prairie hay a foot or two deep. This area isn't called the sandhills just for effect.

It took us several days to complete the transaction and get our calves to town and loaded on freight cars. Then with some other cattle buyers, the brakeman and the conductors, we climbed into the caboose and headed back to Glidden. The caboose, in those days at least, had a coal-burning stove bolted down out in the middle of the car. Benches lined either side along with a chair and a little table for the conductor to use as his "office." It took us two nights and a day, as I recall. Clyde and I, along with our fellow passengers, would take turns stretching out on the benches for a nap as we jolted along, picking up a sandwich whenever the train stopped within range of a beanery. Usually the caboose was a half mile out of town when there was any need to stop.

Was it a long trip? Was going to the moon a long trip for the astronauts?

Our three cars were "set off" on the siding in Glidden. We bucked the cars up to the chutes at the stockyards and unloaded our calves. We went home, got our horses, came back, and drove

100

our cattle back to the feedyards—part of the way through town. Just like Wood Lake!

Now calves are bought either at a private treaty or at a sale barn out in Wood Lake; a fleet of semitrailers is waiting; within hours is loaded and rolling toward the feed lot. The buyers drive comfortably back home in heated and air-conditioned cars. Too bad for kids now!

The Ultimate: To Chicago with Fat Cattle

IF YOU LIVED anywhere in the central Corn Belt, Omaha or Chicago were the only two places to sell fat cattle. Chicago was, of course, the "Hog Butcher for the World"—so said Carl Sandburg. And it was the Ultimate.

Dad always "hit" for the Monday market with much careful watching of the market news for weeks and days before. But finally the sign was right. The cattle were "ready," meaning carrying enough fat. More corn was not adding to their "finish," or we were out of corn and buying didn't seem to make sense. Or, we wanted to get them sold before threshing started.

So plans were made to ship some Saturday night. Always Saturday night because that hit the Monday market. So a car or two was ordered set off at the Glidden siding and we had to go to the depot to make out a bill of lading along with some other paper work.

Then Saturday midafternoon, with a neighbor or Uncle Clyde to help, we would begin driving the cattle downtown. Some of us went ahead to close the neighbors' gates and make sure they turned at the right corner. We tried to move them as slowly as possible to avoid "shrink"; even though it was only a mile, a fat steer unused to exercise loses a lot of pounds in a hurry when he starts to move around. And one of the mysteries of a steer's chemistry is that he tends to bloat when he takes unaccustomed exercise.

Anyway, with dog, men, and boys, the cattle were driven into the stockyards. Then the car had to be "spotted."

The railroad simply shunted the car or cars onto the siding.

101

But in some manner they had to be moved over and lined up with the chute. Moving a boxcar is a bit of an assignment. Dad was always proud he had a team that could do it. It was not that the car was so heavy a team couldn't move it. But few teams had the temperament or training to simply lay into the collar and slowly and gently move a big, nearly immobile object. Most would make one pull and when nothing moved they would start jumping or simply quit. Finally, we would take a kind of pinch bar, slide it under a wheel, and inch the car into position. With the cattle watered and quieted down, everyone went home to supper. Then we all hurried back to load.

Along in early evening the cattle train would come in from the west. It was a local at that point and would stop at every town where cattle were to be picked up. Later it would turn into a through train, stopping only at "division points" for coal, water, and to change crews.

At Glidden it would stop, back onto the siding, pick up our cattle and any others that might be on hand, and move on to the next town. If it were known that a good run of cattle was moving to Chicago, there might be a "cattlemen's car" hitched on just ahead of the caboose. This was a day coach which had seen better days (much better) on a passenger run. The train would arrive at the Chicago stockyards Sunday evening. Each man checked on his cattle as they were unloaded and consigned to a particular commission firm. The cattle were fed and watered and Dad and other shippers would go off to some hotel in the stockyards area.

Early the next morning they would be back to check in with the commission man assigned to their cattle, although actually they couldn't do much about events at that point. The market opened up 50 cents or, more likely, down 50 cents (or so it always seemed) and the buyers on horses went from yard to yard; always mounted; quietly, quizzically moving the cattle around and finally making a bid.

The question was whether to accept it or not. Dad or any other small feeder had little to contribute at that time. The commission man would advise, perhaps holding out to get some other offers. One could always consider the possibility of "holding them over." But that was quite a risk: it was costly; the cattle had to be fed and watered; they might shrink some more; and the offers on Tuesday might be even less satisfactory.

102

At "division points"—every hundred miles or so—locomotives
had to stop to take on fresh supplies of coal and water,
the vital ingredients of steam.

103

So generally the cattle were sold by noon. Dad would go to the commission office in the central stockyards to "settle up." Later that afternoon or evening he would catch a passenger day coach back to Glidden on a "cattleman's pass."

This was a big deal—the whole operation. In the first place this was the ultimate sale of a big share of the corn crop and a gamble taken with a big investment in cattle. A lot was riding on this trip. Furthermore, the trip was an adventure no matter how often it was made, although for Dad it was usually only once or twice a summer at most. He was a small feeder, maybe two or three carloads.

But there was the trip itself, the other people on the train, the comments about crops and prices in other areas "farther east." Then, if railroads fascinated a person at all, and they did most, just the making up the train, changing the crews, switching at the big switchyards in Chicago, eating at the "division points" with the trainmen, "hotboxes," train lingo, and meeting a familiar face from a previous trip, all were exciting. In Chicago we would meet some of the commission men whose names appeared on all their market newsletters. Important people, or so they seemed. Naturally they made over a customer a good deal; they wanted his business. The trip was good for days of table conversation.

In Chicago, downtown was too big and overwhelming, and far too far from the stockyards. Dad usually just went from the yards to the station and caught a train home. But Omaha, when he went there occasionally, was different. He knew his way around that town and would visit a store where I am sure that he found it difficult—given the hard times that prevailed—to "find something to bring home." I remember phonograph records, among other things. One time he intrigued us all by getting off the train in Carroll carrying a little paper container of the kind that we used to get oysters in. He said nothing about it and when we got home after dark he went down and dumped the contents of the container in the stock tank.

104

It was a pair of goldfish which by the next summer had grown to great size. Nature's way had a big thing in that tank. We had hundreds, yea many hundreds of goldfish. We gave them away. The horses drank them. And still there were goldfish in that tank all winter and through another summer or two.

PART FIVE WHAT TO DO

WITH ALL THAT SPARE TIME?

There Wasn't Much

No RADIO; no television! Telephone sporadic and inadequate! What did people do with their spare time? Well, there wasn't much. Certainly "he" didn't putter around in his basement workshop or "she" didn't organize a bridge club just to soak up boredom. Furthermore, something called "the work ethic" tended to "drive" people when they had no other compelling reason. A country club was almost a place of sin. Why, people played golf there—and at 4 o'clock in the afternoon!

Farm hours, of course, were from daylight until dark or longer and the 10-hour, 6-day work week in the factories was just beginning to give way, grudgingly on the part of most management. Labor was cheap and the hours were long in this era. Not just in the factories but on the land. Labor had to be cheap when Dad, his hired man, and his boy would stop their teams, lean back, and uncover a single hill of corn that might have been covered by the cultivator! The Populists contend we became a great nation on a cheap labor, cheap food concept. I catch myself thinking of that when these profusely illustrated foundation reports come to my desk. They tell about the good things foundations are doing. That they are. But the resources they sprinkle around the country and the world were generated too frequently by long hours, plus sweat, toil, tears, and unbelievably grinding poverty on the part of the laboring man and his family. We should bear that in mind when we grow restless with "labor's demands."

On most farms the words vacation, leisure time, and recreation were hardly known. "A trip" was to the state fair, possibly to stay overnight, sleeping in a borrowed tent with blanket spread over a bale of straw for a mattress.

Still, people were not social or political vegetables for all their isolation and relative remoteness and preoccupation with making ends meet! They were eager, some of them at least, for information. What else would motivate a family to go by horse and buggy or spring wagon 10 miles, one way, to a chautauqua program or to "hear a good speech"?

They read, too. What? Well, you can bet it was the *Saturday Evening Post*. From there on it was likely to be the *American, Good Housekeeping, Ladies' Home Journal*. Also, at our house at least, *The Iowa Homestead* or *Wallaces Farmer, The Breeder's Gazette, Capper's Weekly* (from Kansas), *The Drover's Journal* and the *Angus Journal*; in addition, the *American Boy* and the *Youth's Companion*. Naturally, we took the *Glidden Graphic* and the *Des Moines Register*.

Oh yes, the *National Geographic* was in our home, too, in a format surprisingly similar to the present magazine but with much less color, of course.

A look at the *Post* is interesting. It claimed to be "Neutral in Politics, Devoted to Morality, Pure Literature, Foreign and Domestic News, Agriculture, the Commercial Interests, Science, Art and Amusement." It was all of those things, although its "neutrality in politics" would certainly be open to challenge! It just happened to find its political tendencies and those of Big Business to be one and the same. Many of its major stories featured the accomplishments of "the nation's builders." It wasn't accused of being the elite or effete eastern press.

The *Post* was in my parent's home from the time I can remember until it went out of existence in the 1960s. Through thick and thin, it stayed!

Books? Yes, some; by Zane Grey. But mostly magazines and newspapers. On Sunday afternoon we played the Victrola.

Dad liked "Beautiful Ohio," "The Stars and Stripes Forever," "Blue Danube Waltz." On one of his "cattle trips" he brought home a piece of ragtime, "Yes, She's My Elsie Schultzenhein."

I suppose there must have been twenty or thirty records which we moved around from place to place and played and played and played on the big old upright Victrola. Not to my recollection was there a classic in the bunch. But neither was there any "country music."

108

The thing I remember most vividly was the absolute necessity of changing needles after each record. The needles were steel and one side of one record, or at most both sides, was their capacity. They must have been cheap or we wouldn't always have had a fresh supply. The 78 RPM records played only 3–4 minutes. Changing needles and records was a full-time job.

Then along in the early twenties came an utterly unbelievable development that was to change people's lives and make this "one nation indivisible." This country is too big to have a "national newspaper" and the news magazines didn't come along until the thirties. This new thing was something called radio, and then, innocent as the people were of the wonders which scientists were to unloose upon us in such dazzling array in the years to come, they could hardly believe that a person could talk in Pittsburgh, Pennsylvania, and be heard "clear as day"—as the saying went, but actually only at night—away out here in Iowa!

Why Pittsburgh? Because the Westinghouse Company chose Pittsburgh as the place to build one of the very first transmitters in this country. It was called KDKA and everyone with a receiver could and did get KDKA at night. KDKA literally "filled up" the airwaves; it just turned its message loose and it would travel the airways to Iowa. For technical reasons, which are beside the point here, radio signals travel farther at night.

So down at the store, the next morning, the conversation would go, "I got KDKA real good last night," or, "That Florida station really came in strong." It was like bragging about miles per gallon on your new car.

Soon more stations came on the air and then networks—the Red and the Blue. Shortly people on both coasts and all points in between were listening to the same programs and telling and retelling the same jokes. The country was bound together as never before by such names as Amos 'n Andy, Fibber McGee and Molly, the Charlie McCarthy Show, the Cliquo Club Eskimos, the Atwater Kent Hour, and Ma Perkins.

These and others, Aimee Semple McPherson, Ed Wynn, Walter Winchell, Fred Allen, Kate Smith, and a fellow named Norman Baker down at Muscatine who used radio to suggest that transferring goat glands to humans would cure cancer, all became household words.

Amos 'n Andy were so popular factories rearranged their schedules in order that workers need not miss the show. Calvin

109

Coolidge is reported to have advised his staff: "Don't bother me during Amos 'n Andy." The show was piped into theaters so that the audience could listen and keep abreast of this black-face comedy before the silent movie took up! Amos 'n Andy tripled the sales of a toothpaste they advertised! Radio had that kind of a wallop. In 1922, through the sixty national stations, Atwater Kent sold 2 million battery-operated sets.

In the beginning, of course, in the crystal sets, not even a battery was necessary. The crystal set was so simple as to be almost unbelievable. Essentially it consisted of a crystal diode attached to a tuning coil. Such a coil was nothing more than fine copper wire wound around a cardboard tube, maybe an inch or so in diameter. By hitching this all together, in the most elementary manner, and attaching an earphone, quite satisfactory reception was accomplished. You tuned in on a station by moving a thin strip of brass back and forth across the wire-covered tube. You could buy them or you could build your own very easily.

Later came dials you adjusted and readjusted, straining to hear the words or music from some distant station.

Grandma Heaton "enjoyed poor health"—she really did. So to help her while away the hours on her couch, the family splurged and got her one of the first sets with earphones. Alice and I would go there and divide one set of earphones, each having a unit to hold up to our ears. The Hamiltons, for themselves, wouldn't be the first to buy any new gadget like that. But when we did get one it was with a speaker.

In 1928 we were herded into the high school gym to hear Herbert Hoover give his inaugural address. Hoover wasn't exactly a stand-up comedian and given the pitiful reception—from the standpoint of fidelity—I recall the event as being a total disaster. The teachers didn't try anything like that again!

At "the college" the electrical engineers were pretty intrigued with this whole idea, of course, and quite early in the twenties the Iowa State station, WOI, went on the air. Shortly a fellow named Andy Woolfries was known throughout the state, while down at Shenandoah those two great hucksters for nursery stock—Earl May and Henry Field—were soon behind their microphones (their own, KMA and KFNF) selling strawberry plants as well as providing entertainment. Earl May's "schooltime" program along in late afternoon, a bushel of corn-pone foolishness, always brought my Dad to the kitchen during the winter months. He really liked

110

that show. The stations and the business they represented were highly competitive and you were either "for Earl" or "for Henry." We were for Earl, all the way! Didn't like "Old Henry" at all!

Thus from the early twenties on, this invention called radio began to fill in what we now refer to as leisure time. And difficult as it may be for some of the older generation to remember, television oriented as we are today, radio was the national means of communication until after World War II.

Came D Day and the tension of the long military buildup for the invasion of Europe was at hand. Ed Murrow, as only Ed Murrow could do, brought goose pimples, a catch in the throat, a tear in the eye as he read General Eisenhower's initial Order of the Day. America and the world listened:

> Soldiers, sailors and airmen of the Allied Expeditionary Forces, you are about to embark on a great crusade . . . you will bring about the destruction of the German war machine . . . security for ourselves . . . your task will not be an easy one . . . the tide has turned. . . . Good luck and let us all beseech the blessing of the Almighty God upon this great and noble undertaking.

The long-awaited crossing had begun.

That night President Roosevelt told America:

> In this poignant hour, I ask you to join me in a prayer. Almighty God, our sons, pride of our nation, this day have set upon a mighty endeavor, a struggle to preserve our Republic, our religion, our civilization and to set free a suffering humanity. . . . Lead them straight and true; give strength to their arms, stoutness to their hearts. . . . Some will never return. Embrace these, Father, and receive them, Thy heroic servants, into Thy Kingdom of God.

The prayer was long and ended with these words: "Thy will be done, Almighty God, Amen."

Every network carried the message. There were few dry eyes in America that night. Curtis Mitchell in his *Cavalcade of Broadcasting*, 1966, described this as "broadcasting's finest hour" and recalls, "On that night, America was united as never before."

That was radio, a great powerful national and international force—two decades after KDKA! America had no more isolated areas. And between KDKA in Pittsburgh and the end of World War II a surprising amount of spare time developed in no time at all.

The Fourth of July

THE OLD-TIME FOURTH OF JULY, before the prohibition of public sale of fireworks, reminded me of popping corn. The firecrackers began to go off, one or two at a time, a good many days before the Fourth. The rate of explosions increased gradually until the lid would go off on the actual day. Then, as with the corn popper, you could hear a few spasmodic explosions on the fifth, the sixth, and then they would peter out.

Everyone had fireworks. Roman candles, skyrockets, torpedoes, and firecrackers ranging from little 1-inchers that came in packages of fifty or so, with their fuses all woven together, up to big, powerful 3- and 4-inch jobs!

Weren't they dangerous? You bet they were. Every year some eyes would be put out, some fingers blown off, and a few isolated buildings burned down as a result of some fireworks incident.

Then one year someone dropped a match in the fireworks display in one of the stores in Spencer, up in northwest Iowa, and in short order the entire main street of that major county seat town was in ashes. That was it. Civilization began to close in and another freedom—to burn up or to blow up—was gone.

But before that, oh boy! As soon as Tom Roberts laid in the supply in his corner drugstore we began to accumulate for our own special celebration. Dad entered into the spirit of this activity with as much enthusiasm as any of the kids. He loved fireworks and even after they were outlawed in Iowa, he would stop and pick up a few in Missouri if they happened to be on sale. After all, restricting fireworks was going just a little too far, even though he was about as law-abiding a citizen as I ever knew.

With stock laid in, I would experiment with a few ahead of time, but most were saved for the Fourth. Either in town at a celebration or just around home, we would concentrate on putting 3- and 4-inchers under tin cans to see how high they would blow. Pretty high, too. High as the house. Lots of power in those big crackers. Torpedoes, powered with a slingshot or just heaved up against a building, would explode with a real bang and send the chickens scattering.

Also, I remember tossing out some of those little 1-inchers after they were lit. The chickens, accustomed to being fed corn,

112

thought they were some new nutritional package. They rushed up and the lucky bird ran off with the prize just about the time that it went off with a bang. That chicken had a real surprised look! It survived, although its interest in such activity was understandably dulled.

It seemed as though night would never come but it did, finally, and all was ready. Our cousins, the Riches, would be there and Dad would have gone to some little effort to build a trough from which to launch the skyrockets. Eventually, it was dark enough and kids, sparkler size and up, would gather around for their turn at helping launch the display.

It was always out in the front yard, with all items aimed away from the buildings. Precautions were taken. But always some younger member of the cousin tribe would get excited and forget to let go of a firecracker after it was lit, or would swing a belching Roman candle around wildly and send all parties scrambling for safety.

Accidents were minor, though, and finally, with sadness, the last skyrockets would light up the sky and burst with a great flowering effect. The smoke would drift lazily off across the humid countryside. Everyone would sit around and talk for a while, have some homemade ice cream, and the Riches would head for home.

The Fourth was over. (Of course, I always laid a few firecrackers aside for an emergency!)

Chautauqua Came to the Country

IF YOU LOOK under "Extension Service" in the encyclopedia you will find two words that are almost totally lost from present dialogue—lyceum and chautauqua. The encyclopedia man sees lyceum and chautauqua as forerunners of the present-day efforts of major universities to "extend" their services to adult participants.

Lyceum came first and chautauqua was a phenomenon of the Midwest—and many other regions—during the first three decades of this century.

113

Aside from its massive grain elevator, Ralston is just about as small a town as can stay in business in Iowa. Its population is 129. It was never much different. Yet "good speakers" would come to Ralston in the World War I era and farmers would drive in for miles around, both with horse and buggy and earliest autos, to attend. Mother doesn't recall what organized effort brought this about, but it was a lyceum-like effort of some kind. She does recall going with horse and spring wagon to Jefferson, a trip of 10 miles or so, to attend chautauqua programs.

Again she emphasizes the "good speakers." Today, if a "good speaker" comes on radio or television, we are more likely to flick him off. The idea of spending a day and half the night driving off across country with a horse-drawn rig to "hear a good speaker" is beyond comprehension.

Until the Depression put chautauquas and a lot of other things out of business, they were a big thing in the small towns of the Midwest. The institution flourished for perhaps 30 years or so and during that time chautauqua week was something to take precedent over almost anything else going on in town.

It was concerts, it was lectures, it was drama, it was entertainment, it was education—all "live" right there under the big tent on the school grounds or city park. The seats were planks set on building blocks. In the afternoon the heat was intense and only slightly less so in the evenings. The customers came, fanned themselves, drank "ice cold lemonade, 5 cents," and applauded or hissed as the occasion demanded.

Generally the program was intended to entertain or "leave a message." It was what the media people now call a "magazine format." One evening's program would likely include a lecture, always some music, a dramatic skit, and some audience singing. No one read the ads (I don't recall any—everyone just knew when chautauqua came to town) to determine whether the program was going to be XXX, R, or GP; they were good solid early twentieth-century Methodist all the way! As a matter of fact, chautauqua as an institution, before it took to the road under tents, began as a means of training Sunday school teachers! It was strictly family entertainment.

In Blair, according to Ruth, the last day was home talent day. Kids would spend all week rehearsing for their part in the final program.

Because chautauqua was a "good thing for a town" Granddad

114

Heaton would buy tickets just to help assure its success. That was one way to get in. Otherwise there was water to be carried from the city park pump backstage where 10-year-old boys were entranced with the performers so casually donning makeup, wigs, and costumes for their acts.

Under the impact of the Depression and radio, chautauqua folded its tent for the last time along about 1930.

A vestige remains in Red Oak, Iowa, where chautauqua was such an institution that a pavilion was provided to house the event. Now with a rekindling of interest in such things, this aging structure has been designated as a point of historical worth and is being restored. It stands in Red Oak Chautauqua Park!

But chautauqua was a boon, while it lasted, to entertainment-starved midwesterners.

The Jeffery, the Reo, and a New Chevrolet

THE FIRST CAR my folks had was a 1914 Jeffery. In one of the innumerable mergers and mutations that occurred in early auto companies, the Jeffery years later became first the Nash and then the Rambler. The 1914 model was by no means the earliest car on the road. But it was an early one. As I look back upon it my folks must have rather splurged for that time. It was quite a massive monster, remembered particularly because it had four forward speeds. Most of the time Dad was quite satisfied with the third speed. But on occasion, with a great clashing of gears, Dad would shift over in fourth, mainly when he seemed to be in a kind of carefree mood (which was not often; Dad's times were not usually carefree) and we would seem to be nearly flying along. I suppose it was maybe 40 or 50 miles per hour.

It had side curtains, of course, and was started with a crank, usually pretty responsively.

I don't recall the exact circumstances which caused the Jeffery to give way to the Reo for the Reo was very nearly of the same vintage. But I do remember that when we traded the Jeffery, it went directly to the junkyard in Carroll and Mother "felt badly" when she heard they had gone to work on it with sledgehammers and blowtorches. Material things meant more then.

I learned to drive the Reo and cobbled up some kind of an extension on the foot accelerator so that I could reach it. The main thing I recall about that car was how much better it performed in the evening. The way it would purr along in the dusk as compared to its performance during the heat of the day was very, very noticeable. The cool or the dampness of the evening air did something to the carburetor mix that made evening driving a joy.

Eventually the Reo became a real problem. It would "heat up" even on the shortest drives. We would have to carry some extra water along and then the car would get so hot you couldn't get near enough to get at the radiator and give it a cooling drink.

So, even though I am sure it was a great financial strain, Dad began to shop for a new car. This was a move undertaken very reluctantly because of the fear of being harassed by car salesmen. Then, the word that a person was considering such a purchase would bring a salesman or salesmen who wouldn't take a "no." They were as desperate to sell the car as the buyer was reluctant to buy. The aggressive salesman might make two or three calls a day. The salesman we bought our first new car from was—a preacher! I think he had a church in Ralston and he was no doubt starving to death. I remember his following Dad out to the barn at milking time and giving his sales pitch as Dad proceeded with the chore at hand. Dad milked; the preacher talked. And he made a sale; a Chevrolet Landau, 1926.

We lived on the "Black place" north of Ralston when that transaction occurred. We drove the old Reo to Scranton where the trade was to take place and as we pulled up by the garage the old Reo was so hot we feared it might fly completely to pieces. With steam shooting out of all its cracks and crevices, it was so hot the motor kept right on running after the ignition was off. Fearing the garage owner would come out and see it in this sad state, we simply went off and left it clanging away, a kind of death rattle, and got our new Chevrolet.

At home the next day I remember Mother and I went out and sat in the new car and marveled at its comforts, fingered all the gadgets, and enjoyed the new car smell. Its acquisition was a really major event. And of course it could not be driven over 20 miles per hour for the first 1,000 miles. It had to be "broken in." When you saw a car almost creeping along the road, you knew someone had bought a new car. It was an event because cars weren't being shucked off then every time some designer came out with a new model.

117

A Standoff: Granddad Versus the Model T

WELL OVER 100 different makes of American autos have been on the road at one time or another. But none made its mark in history like the famed Model T, 1909–1927. It was, of course, the first car to be really mass produced. But it had other unique characteristics.

By present-day standards, or almost any standards, it rattled, vibrated, shook, and shimmied. Those who now prefer the stick shift so that they will have the experience of "really driving" would have been totally enamored with the Model T; the driver and the machine were as one.

The driver clutched the wheel with both hands, only giving up the grip on the right hand briefly to adjust the hand throttle which was a lever protruding much as the turn lever protrudes on modern cars. The car was light, quick, and high. The slightest turn of the steering wheel seemed to be transmitted tenfold and instantly to the front wheels.

It was this kind of machine Granddad Heaton learned to drive when he was probably well past 50. It was a crank job, of course, with a wire loop sticking out of the radiator to provide whatever choking might be necessary, usually considerable. Granddad would first make all the minute adjustments: gas and spark with the two levers attached to the steering column, then the crank and choke.

(The Model T was famous for "kicking" and breaking the arms of those who were not experienced, as well as some who were. The cautious and the smart usually satisfied themselves with a simple upstroke. If this failed to do the job, and it frequently did, the temptation was to "spin it." Then at some point in the effort there was a tendency for the engine to backfire and drive the crank suddenly counterclockwise. A broken arm was the frequent result. Also, if the beast was particularly stubborn, it sometimes helped to jack up one hind wheel. As you cranked, the wheel would swing into action and add some momentum to the cranking effort.)

But there was Granddad, coordinating the two levers and the choke and cranking all at the same time. All this was pretty perplexing to him and not infrequently the car would fire a time or two but die before he could race around to make proper ad-

118

justments of the levers at the steering wheel, first spark and then gas. So his tendency was, following each failure, to advance the gas lever a little more. Shortly it was all the way open. At that point the car would start with a loud explosion and the chickens would scurry for cover, the dogs would bark, and the windows would rattle. Whereupon he would race back to the driver's seat and in his frenzy cut the gas back to the point where the engine would fail. And then the process was repeated all over again.

But under the best of circumstances, Granddad kept the motor running at about 95 percent of capacity, either when the car was standing still (as still as a Model T would stand) or when in flight. I often think of that car when I see a workman using a jackhammer on a road job.

Given that kind of acceleration and the unique manner in which power was transmitted from engine to wheels Granddad usually went from a standing start to about 10 miles an hour in about 10 feet, or so it seemed.

He was known to have lost control of the car, ending up in the ditch. But—right side up! Without ever changing the rate of acceleration, he would race down the ditch for a way, steer back up onto the road, and whiz on as though he had planned it that way all the time.

Eventually he had a sedan but still a Model T. Once, because he was about out of gas, he was hurrying home with 50 pounds of ice in the car. He hurried too fast and turned over at a corner. With a little help, he removed the ice, turned the car back on its wheels, reloaded the ice, and proceeded on his way.

Fords were especially susceptible to stalling when going up hills. Something about the relation of the gas tank, which was under the front seat, and the motor. This could be overcome by backing up the hills. This was a practice followed by many Ford owners, Granddad Heaton included.

Somewhat the same effect could be had by simply putting some air pressure on the gas tank. Some folks had an arrangement where they would hook the tire pump to the gas tank and build up some pressure if they couldn't make it over the hill. Granddad didn't have anything as sophisticated. But on occasion his passengers would be asked to provide the pressure. The opening on the gas tank was under the right side of the front seat. The passenger would take out the seat, get down on his knees, and for all he was worth blow into the gas tank. It would work.

119

I did it once on the famed Bolton Hill. This little hill on the Greene–Carroll County line going up out of the Raccoon River valley was the testing ground; it was a good car that would make it on high. In Granddad's Model T you were glad to make it at all.

The lights on the Model T were a strictly magneto job, no battery. The intensity of the lights was in relation to the speed of the car, the faster you went the better the lights. Mr. Nader would not have considered this ideal from a safety standpoint. But it could be nicely overcome by simply driving in low gear: slow car speed; high engine speed; better lights.

Then, as now, there were different makes of autos, but a surprising (well, maybe not so surprising) similarity of design.

120

Life and Romance Revolved around Trains

ALAS, they are no more—steam locomotives, country depots, and the unreality of a sleek, super passenger train, lights ablaze, gliding off across an otherwise dark countryside.

In the best years of my young life the farm we operated lay for a full mile along the main line of the North Western just west of Glidden. The trains were a part of our life.

We knew their numbers. Number 16 was a passenger from the west and it was due in Glidden at about 7 in the evening. We were usually at the supper table or hurrying in that direction. We could see it come out of the west and someone never failed to comment, "Sixteen is right on the dot," or "Sixteen is running a little late." So it was with the other dozen or so passenger trains that went within a quarter of a mile of our house every day.

The better trains, transcontinentals, that carried such distinctive names as the Portland Rose and the Challenger (San Francisco or L.A.), went by our place at night, some about bedtime. They would go streaking along, coach and first-class cars fully lighted, seemingly totally detached from the mundane world of the countryside. Tomorrow they would be in Denver, then Salt Lake City, and the second morning "at the Coast." What romance!

When the great heavy locomotive would go pounding down the track at night, shafts of light from the firebox would dart out over the tender each time the fireman pulled open the door to heave in another shovelful of coal. There were lots of shafts of light, and a lot of coal thrown in. The fireman earned his money. But that all added to the excitement, action, and life.

The front-end brakeman, known always as the "brakie," sat on one side of the cab, helping the engineer keep an eye on the track. But the captain of the ship (even though the conductor, even on a freight, is in charge) was the engineer. He was a much more visible person than those who today drive the diesels. He wore an engineer's cap, a red handkerchief around his neck, and goggles. But he would still wave at a boy plowing corn. That made the boy's day.

I would try always to have my corn plow as near the track as possible when a train was coming through. Because the loss of a few corn plants was not unimportant, Dad always suggested that I just stop and watch the train when it was going by; not try to plow and watch at the same time.

Among the other trains going through was the "stub." It was the local that went one way each day on our "division." It stopped at every station, taking passengers to the next town or to some division point to catch a through train. But it also carried a baggage car plus only one or two coaches, hence, the "stub." It had a light engine with high-drive wheels which made it possible to develop high speeds quickly, but gave it little pulling power. It didn't need power; it needed to go fast between stops, and it did!

Trains also had another kind of passenger no longer to be found—and all to the good—hoboes! Many a freight would have as many as fifty men riding on top of the boxcars, inside any open cars, and sometimes hanging on between cars. So many rode during hard times that the railroad dicks could not begin to drive them away. These men were destitute and out of work. They didn't know where they were going, but it was always to something better.

Under the railroad bridge over a little stream at the back of our farm and in a little draw full of willows along the fence we frequently found evidences where one or more of these travelers had dropped off to spend the night or make some coffee around a little brush fire. Actually, however, few of these men ever stopped off. Mother was worried they would and she dreaded to see an unidentified man coming down the road on foot. She was afraid of them, and it was an accepted fact that if you fed one of these tramps he would leave some kind of sign at the lane gate and others would stop knowing this was a soft touch.

Other personalities along the track were the men in the section crews. We knew most of them and would visit when they worked along our farm. These work trains had maybe 100 or so men, frequently Mexicans, who would live in "work cars" parked along the siding near our farm while they replaced rails and re-laid ballast. This was tough, hard work, all done mechanically now, or nearly so. Then, the roadbeds were kept in A 1 shape. Two or three times each summer a great burner would go up the track and with blazing flame that reached from one side of the track to the other would do away with any weeds that might be showing up.

Many of the trains, but not all, would stop in Glidden. Being there at the depot when the train came in was a major event. The most incredible feature, insofar as passenger trains were concerned, was the dining cars. We would stand and look in those dining car windows in absolute awe: white tablecloths; a rose on the table by the window. Waiters in white coats served elegant ladies and gentlemen seeming to take such utter out-of-this-world extravagance quite for granted. The idea of not packing a lunch for a train trip never occurred to us. And the idea of anyone wealthy enough to buy food on the train was beyond comprehension.

The depot, too, with its potbellied stove and its unique smell (where did that come from?) is something that never failed to offer intrigue. The station agent, green eyeshade and all, busily made magic on the Morse code key which clicked along endlessly by the bay window where a man could watch both ways and carry on a conversation, through his fingers, with some remote area. He would come over to sell a ticket and then break away to go back to his key and give it a few knowing taps. Utter mystery; and he did it so casually. "Yes, 16 has left Denison—but it may have to lay over in Carroll."

But finally it would come, slowing down evenly as it approached the station platform where passengers and the curious gathered. The engineer, from that mighty throne, would study the crowd with friendly interest as he brought the great beast to a stop.

No jet plane will ever replace that scene or the excitement it brought to those who could literally reach out and touch that huge source of power.

Engines were of different types or "series." We knew them all. Alas, the best, the biggest and the heaviest freights, were the last to be built before technology put them out of business. All of them, of course, could run only a certain distance, about 100 miles between division points, without taking on coal and water. Even that was exciting.

Trains would break down, of course. We knew all the lingo: a "hotbox," or a "pulled coupling." The most exciting thing that ever occurred and right at our farm within a few hundred yards of the house, was to have one of the biggest engines tip over!

Located along our farm was a siding where freights would wait while passengers passed. This particular freight was pulling out when, through some malfunction, the frog on the switch

123

didn't open. It was there as a protective device to keep an engine on the siding from sliding out in front of or into a passing train. The protection was to derail the intruder. In this case the frog did that so successfully that the engine not only left the tracks but rolled over on its side and eventually onto its back right on the end of our cornfield. Fire, steam, coal, and men went in all directions. It was major in every sense of the word. Fortunately no one was hurt. But day and night work crews worked under flood lights around the clock to right the engine and get it on the track. This all happened in the dead of winter and a blizzard, and the excitement of seeing this operation firsthand was a new first for a family whose life revolved around trains in a large way.

For me the romance of trains was to go on. I frequently went back and forth to college via train as did almost everyone else. I remember particularly having Dad get up and take me to Carroll, 8 miles to the west, to catch an early morning train to Ames. This would be a through train and many of the passengers including families of all ages and sizes would have ridden it together for hundreds of miles, perhaps from "the Coast." By mid-America they were firm friends, having watched each other's kids, and probably shared each other's lunches, perhaps for two days and nights.

At 5 in the morning every seat was taken, either by an upright person or more likely by those stretched out across two seats or by children dead to the world. All were sleep-sodden. None wished to be roused or wakened. Even those stretched out across the two seats, asleep or feigning sleep, ignored the newcomer venturing onto their claim.

I wasn't very popular. I would stand in the aisle until the conductor came by to pick up my ticket. He then might shake someone into a degree of civility and indicate a seat for the newcomer. But I still wasn't popular.

Just prior to and during World War II when I was doing my stint in Washington, I suddenly found I was riding in those Pullman cars that went gliding off across a darkened countryside

124

These engines are of the kind that thundered across the country pulling freights over transcontinental lines like Union Pacific and Chicago and North Western. The lower rig was just under 100 feet and carried 22 tons of fuel! They vanished shortly after World War II. The North Western ran for a mile along our Glidden farm and a wave from an engineer would bring a chill of excitement to a teen-age boy.

at night and had so fascinated me as a boy on the farm. It was the overnight trips on the B and O's Capitol Limited that took me so often into another world.

On the run from Chicago to Washington it left the windy city about 5 in the afternoon from Grand Central Station, a huge, cavernous, barnlike structure, about as unhomey a place as one could imagine. At midday it was still dark and poorly lighted.

You stepped out of that dismal waiting room and there on

the first track was that beautiful train. This too was a poorly lighted area. And so as you walked past the club car it already shone light and bright with the first passengers settling back in the lounge chairs with their evening papers, their cigars, and a drink.

If you were feeling a bit extravagant you paid a little extra out of your own pocket and had a roomette; a room to yourself, complete with washroom. The porter fussed over you and brought you a table to work on if you wanted it. You put your shoes outside the door and they were freshly shined when you woke up the next morning.

But the greatest feeling of all was when the train was loaded, the "All *'board!'*" shout went out, and so gently you hardly knew it was in motion, the train began its run. Shortly it pulled out from under the far end of the train shed and there was a great mixed feeling of power, comfort, security, and coziness, particularly if that cocoon of steel and beauty was driving with increasing speed in the rain. That always seemed to add something— defying the elements in such comfort and security!

No airborne craft will ever provide that particular atmosphere. The contrast was only heightened when, as the evening wore on and Gary's slums and steel mills had given way to rolling countryside, you made your way to the dining car for a dinner of your choice on a par with that you might have ordered at a Chicago restaurant except that it was more leisurely and you were more likely to have a visit with your table companions over pie and coffee.

In the evening you read, caught up on any work that you were carrying along, went to bed (the porter would make up your berth while you were at dinner if you wanted it so), and woke up the next morning at about Harper's Ferry.

Rolling down the Potomac you had breakfast of your choice, time for a second cup of coffee, and a glance at the morning paper put on at Baltimore. You taxied to the office by 9 o'clock.

A not unimportant part of America's gracious living concept left the scene when its people took to wings and all travel was rush, rush, rush!

The Trains at Blair

RUTH FARNHAM HAMILTON WRITES . . .

BLAIR was on a branch of the Chicago and North Western Railroad about 25 miles or a one-hour trip from Omaha. It was far enough from Sioux City, perhaps 75 miles, that I never made that trip. Blair was a "big" town of about 2,500 in the early twenties so we rated a scheduled stop. However, De Soto, 5 miles to the south, had only a station the size of a one-room schoolhouse and a general store with post office at the rear. Such small places rated only a flag stop. In the 25 miles between Blair and Omaha there were two scheduled stops and two flag stops.

As a small child, "good times" revolved around meeting the train at the depot. Fortunately, Blair was located so that with one trip to the depot in the evening, we could see both northbound and southbound trains. The northbound usually sidetracked at Blair to wait for the southbound. It did, that is, unless the station agent received a message via Morse code to indicate that the southbound train was late enough that the northbound could sidetrack at Tekamah, 18 miles to the north, without holding the other one up.

On our trips to see the trains we stood back from the engine with our hands over our ears to dull the noise and our eyes closed to avoid the cinders. Almost always some of our friends would be boarding or deboarding.

Occasionally we would have even a greater adventure with a trip to Omaha for a day of visiting and perhaps a ride on a streetcar. But my fondest memory is of the very occasional trips I would make home for the weekend with Lorraine Seltz. Lorraine attended high school in Blair and roomed next door to us. Lorraine's parents farmed about 6 miles south of Blair but it was impractical for her to attend school in Blair and go home each night. No buses. Early on Monday morning her father drove us to De Soto where the station agent would flag the train to stop, we'd board, ride to Blair, a trip of about 15 minutes and arrive in time for school.

PART SIX   THE LITTLE

When School Buses Used Real Horsepower

WHEN the famed Little Red Schoolhouses (all I ever saw were white) began to give way to what were known as "consolidated" town schools in the twenties, there came the problem of how to get the kiddies to school. When there was a school every 2 miles, they walked. But when it was 10 or 12, that was something else again.

The buses were, like everything else, geared to horsepower. The first bus I rode on was a commercially built rig and pulled by a pair of lanky horses that went on a dead trot from one end of the trip to the other. Dad used to shake his head over this abuse of horseflesh; a horse hitched to a buggy might trot but not a farm horse hitched to a wagon. But trot they did, driven by a couple of high school boys who would stable them in a barn when we arrived in town.

The bus itself was nothing but a wagon-box type of affair, mounted on a high-wheel running gear. It was windowless except at front and rear and the front with a slot through which the driver passed the lines. Benches ran the length of the bus so that the kids sat facing each other.

Solid black side curtains were of course kept rolled down during the winter. In the spring, the next biggest event to going

WHITE SCHOOLHOUSE

129

without your long underwear was when it was possible to roll up the side curtains on the bus. Then you leaned out the open sides, smelled the spring in the air as the vehicle rolled along the countryside, occasionally meeting another horse-drawn rig. Then you forgot about how cold the bus was in the winter or how long it took to get to school, even with the horses at a fast gait.

Then came trucks—just plain farm trucks converted to school buses. Farmers would bid for a bus route and if they were successful would build an arrangement on their stock or grain truck

With consolidation came the horse-drawn rigs that prevailed until about the mid-twenties. My sister and I rode these rigs in both Clay County and at Glidden.

that looked a little like a modern-day camper, at least in profile.

Again benches were tacked up along the walls; maybe one down through the middle. Any windows added were at the discretion of the bidder who would cobble up various methods of rear mounting.

I recall one rear-mounting arrangement particularly well; it had been installed by the Gymer boys who were good mechanics and physically rugged. A joke to them was to electrify (from the truck battery) the iron rod everyone grabbed as they took their first step up and into the bus. They would single out some kid not particularly high on their favorites list and just when he was firmly grasping the bar and had one foot on the lower step, they would touch the button up in the cab. The kid would let out a yowl heard halfway to town, his books would go one direction, his lunch another and, depending on age, he would be reduced to gushing tears or turned into a fighting maniac. The driver would pretend to be totally unaware of what had happened.

The Gymers soon were not bus drivers. They were tough. I can remember them demonstrating the kick their battery would

One of the earliest of the commercially built buses used in Greene County, Iowa. Farmers sometimes would bid on the school route and if successful, would cobble up a homemade cover on the grain box of their farm truck and pick up a few extra dollars hauling the kids.

131

give that iron bar. One of them would grasp the bar and the other would push the button. The brother would hold on and the charge was sharp enough so that he couldn't hold his hand still; his hand and arm would twitch and jump. But he held on, to the utter fascination of his audience.

It was well into the midtwenties before anything approaching present-day school buses began to appear and they frequently were ahead of their times insofar as roads were concerned. It wasn't just a matter of "snow days"; it was mud days in spring and fall when the bus couldn't negotiate the average country roads. A major impetus to getting gravel on country roads was to make it possible for the school bus to get through.

One-room country schools gave way to consolidated schools. This called for transportation for the kiddies, first horse-drawn and then these motorized units in the twenties.

132

Country Schools, 1900: Three Teachers a Year!

INSTRUCTIONAL MATERIALS CENTERS (IMC's) are big in elementary schools these days. They contain every known media for transferring the world's knowledge painlessly and quickly into hopefully pliable minds.

The one-room schoolhouses that dotted Iowa at the turn of the century had a Webster's dictionary and very little else, unless the teacher happened to show unusual initiative. Inasmuch as they usually had a different teacher for each of the three terms, the incentive for even the most dedicated teacher was not great.

It was into that kind of a teaching experience that Mother went at age 16! That was 2 years before any teacher was supposed to meet whatever standards there were. Mother was never quite certain as to how she circumvented the regulations.

She had gone to the schools in Glidden until she was about 9 or 10 when her father's creamery burned down and they moved to a pretty ordinary "river farm" 10 miles northeast of town. She went into country school and followed the usual procedure of not going from one grade to another but when, having "finished one reader" moving automatically to the next. The readers went from the first through the fifth.

When Mother finished the fifth reader, apparently ahead of schedule and with some help at home from her father, she said the "teacher really didn't know what to do with me." So she had Mother help some of the smaller kids "out in the hall."

During the following summer the "normal" (teachers' meeting) was held at Carroll. She took an exam which resulted in her receiving a "permit" (not a certificate, she emphasized) to begin teaching that fall before her 17th birthday.

The governance of the local school district was not a cluttered arrangement. A "director" was elected by the *men* of the district and he hired the teacher. Mother recalls that when her father was the director there would be much traffic in the yard as young girls—and some men—would come to "apply for the school."

Mother was hired by Bob Hamilton, later to be her father-in-law. In the fall term of 10 weeks she drove a horse and buggy from her home to the school night and morning, an 8-mile round trip. Late in the fall she would start from home before daylight, drive the 4 miles, put her horse in a neighbor's barn, go to the schoolhouse, start the fire, light the kerosene lamps, and prepare for the day's activities.

The kids of all ages and sizes would troop into a small center hall, hang their wraps on nails along one wall, and deposit their lunch pails on a bench which also held the water pail and wash basin. They sat two to a double seat. Their equipment was a "reader"--whichever one they were using at the time, a slate, and at some later stages a geography and a math book that stressed the "inductive" method.

The biggest decision of the morning and afternoon was to decide who was to be allowed to go to the nearby farmhouse and bring a pail of water. This was a much sought after assignment; the lucky one got out of studying. The second most fortunate was allowed to "pass the pail" when it was brought back. This student went up and down the aisle, each kid taking a dipperful of water, all of which he was supposed to drink, once having taken it, and then returning the dipper for the use of the next student.

One dipper did for all, sharing not only the cool goodness of the bucket but also any kid distemper that might be present. Oh yes, the kids could dampen their "slate rags" at the same time, thus the better to erase and start over.

By the time the fifth reader was reached the fare was of real substance: Melville and Thoreau. But, as Mother reported, many of those kids came from homes where there was scarcely a book or a paper to be seen. Boys in their teens sounded out one word at a time, the whole operation utterly devoid of meaning.

In the winter term it was too cold to drive and so she boarded, for $3 a week she recalls, with a neighbor near the school. Normally the winter term, which ran for 12 weeks, was taught by a man, if one was to be found. It was in the winter term that the boys, boys big enough to do farm work, came to school. It took a man to handle them!

Others sometimes used the school building. Mother particularly didn't care for one church group; they burned her kindling. So she brought it with her each day.

At another school she taught, the boys worked and worked and built a raft. She was frightened they would put it on the neighboring river and drown. Just when she didn't know where to turn to stop the project, and just as it was virtually complete, providence stepped in. Someone stole the raft.

134

Tenure was no problem. When Bob Hamilton's daughter Josie was out of school, he asked Mother to find another job so Josie could have the school close to home. Mother did, and taught at several other schools. One was only a mile from her home. That was handy; she could walk there.

These country schools were to hang on and, like consolidated schools and reorganization plans, to be in some areas centers of community argument and dispute for half a century. Some argued vigorously for their virtues; for example, how younger children learned from hearing older ones recite. Changes on the farms themselves came more rapidly and with less resistance than changes in the rural schools.

This "facility," which served a rural school in central Iowa in the twenties, obviously discouraged a problem now somewhat prevalent—loitering in the toilet.

Your Treasured Marble Shooter

Fox AND Geese! Crack the Whip! Shooting marbles!

Are these such innocent activities that they no longer excite the fourth- to eighth-grade set? They did in the twenties!

Marble shooting season came on strong in the spring, about the time you shucked your long underwear. Every boy would show up with a big pocket full of assorted marbles, or maybe if he were really a professional, have his collection in a cloth bag with a drawstring top.

Draw a circle in the dirt, get your favorite shooter, and go to work. Some kids developed deadly accuracy and from distances of 3 or 4 feet could blast an opponent's marble clear out of the circle. It meant holding your thumb and tongue just right.

As with many other kid games, I was never very good at marbles. But I was good at "I drops." If you were shooting from a distance of $3\frac{1}{2}$ feet, for instance, you could choose to attempt to drop your marble from that same distance—vertically! That was "I drops."

The typical marble collection had variety. There were "steelies," nothing more than ball bearings from some piece of machinery. Then some cheap clay jobs, not very good, not very much sought after. Also commies and aggies—colored glass jobs. Then, your shooter; your pride and joy. I had one once that was a beauty, a blend of white and cherry red and half again as large as an average marble. It was mottled like a marble cake, a genuine Carnelian. I don't know how I acquired such a prize, probably from a collection in Grandmother Hamilton's attic.

One day, as classes were taking up, I was holding a double handful of my marbles out to show someone across the aisle. Just then a girl widely known for her ability to do somewhat less than totally endearing acts, walked by and batted that whole collection out of my hand.

Marbles went in all directions, off under chairs and desks clear across the room, and just as the teacher walked in! I had no opportunity to undertake retrieval; I was wiped out. My favorite shooter was gone, never to be recovered.

I'm sorry about this, Lord, but I have to admit a little cloud still hung over the memory of that girl when I read her obituary a few years ago. Marbles were important.

136

Fox and Geese was a snow-time game. Certain configurations, in the form of paths, were developed in the new snow. They were like figure eights with wide circles that came close enough together at certain points so the Geese could step from one area to another. The Fox couldn't. But it was complicated enough so that the Fox could, under certain circumstances, corner the Geese.

We played it a lot at noon and recess.

Crack the Whip. How does one describe that broken arm operation? A line of kids would join hands, the leader would start running in one direction, faster and faster and faster, with the line of hand-holding kids trailing along behind. Then the leader would turn in a circle and the physics of the operation was such that the far end of the line had to cover a lot more territory than the lead end so the kids on the far end had to run faster and faster and faster to keep up. Soon their feet were barely touching the ground. Handholds gave way and the line began to disintegrate, a kid at a time. They went catapulting off in all directions—falling, stumbling, tearing clothes, getting grass burns, and occasionally breaking an arm! Don't ask why we played that game!

Class fights between senior- and lower-class boys also took on classic proportions when the sap began to run in the spring of the year.

For seniors it was an attempt to initiate younger boys into the responsibilities that would be theirs in their last year in school. For younger boys, particularly juniors, it was an opportunity to demonstrate they were quite equal to the assignment.

Some were just plain fights. More typically, one group or the other would attempt to separate one or two boys off from his peer crowd and take them, along about midnight, about 12 or 15 miles from Glidden and kick them out on some remote country road. The phone service wasn't very good and no one ever considered stopping in at a darkened farm home to explain the ridiculous predicament into which he had fallen.

So there was a night-long trudge back to town, over rutty or muddy country roads, trying to steer clear of the barking dogs which met the scared kid at every farmstead. He would show up

137

back home about sunup, a pretty bedraggled specimen of young manhood. Parental apprehension varied from home to home, of course, but given the general understanding of what was going on, it was kept within livable bounds.

Oh yes, it added interest to the episode to leave the unlucky victim off in that dark corner of nowhere—without his pants!

Hot Lunches! What's It All Coming To?

SCHOOL LUNCHES, hot and served at school, were beyond comprehension in the 1920s. If anyone had suggested that the federal government should interest itself in adequate noontime snacks for the kiddies, they would have been laughed out of town. No doubt some socialist theory! So the "country kids" all came armed with a paper sack holding a soggy sandwich, an apple, and a mashed up cookie and didn't know they were deprived!

If the weather was fit, even remotely, the boys all headed for some favorite spot behind the building, devoured their sandwiches, and were playing ball by 12:10. If they were confined to the school lunchroom, they had finished by 12:08 (saved the time of going outside) and were playing ball with apples or the cores thereof in the lunchroom (while the flak in the air reduced the lunchroom supervisor to tears).

At that time I could go out behind the schoolhouse, wolf down a peanut butter sandwich in nothing flat, and still be able to spit. Now I can't eat a piece of watermelon without a glass of water!

Granddad Heaton kept bees so we had honey sandwiches sometimes. I remember them well. They would soak completely through and the sandwich would be something like a big candy bar. (Which reminds me of Mother telling of the kids attending her school whose sandwich spread was a mixture of lard and molasses; no oleo, no butter to be had.)

Surprisingly, it wasn't the ingredients of the lunch that caused as much fuss as the container. Those kids whose mothers were satisfied to put their goodies in a sack or wrap them in a

138

newspaper were the lucky ones. Once done with lunch, the kids gave the sack or paper a heave and were ready for action.

But Aunt Jo, our thoughtful maiden aunt, was always thinking of us and our cold lunches. So she was always buying us lunch boxes; big ones. They would hold a thermos bottle in the lid. In bulk they were about the size of a tackle box and weighed about as much! How we hated them. Once empty they had to be returned to a locker. That took time away from playing ball. And you had to remember to take them home on the bus. What an impediment. Also, they were kind of sissy. But, some families had maiden aunts.

Long Underwear Was Not an Ego Builder

SPRING DIDN'T COME with the robins. It arrived, officially, when Mother finally relented and agreed that the kids could go to school without their long underwear: union-suit type, full-legged, full-armed, and with a convenient drop seat!

139

They never fit. Why the underwear always seemed too big, with kids growing the way they do, I don't know. But it seemed to stretch. So there was always a baggy handful of battleship gray pushing out around a kid's shirt cuffs. (I am always reminded of that unhappy situation now when I see some dandy wearing ruffled cuffs with his dinner jacket!)

The ankles particularly stretched. So at shoe top, no matter how carefully you folded them over in the morning and tried to pull stockings up over them with some neatness, the place where the foot bone joined the leg bone appeared as though it had been handcrafted by a disenchanted troll using spare parts from the salvage yard. All the kids wore long underwear. But some kind of social stigma still attached to the obvious evidence of long underwear at all four corners of each kid.

So, with the first signs of spring the clamor began to put aside this cocoon of inconvenience and social discomfort. The period of debate went on for some weeks. Weather was on the side of the kids and finally came the day. No sensation ever quite duplicated that shiver when you stepped outside some really quite brisk April morning and felt a fresh breeze rush up your pants legs clear to your crotch. You had to admit it was a little brisk. But you didn't mention that. Because you were free.

Winter was over!

Of Course You Had to Eat after School

BY AND LARGE, everyone rode the school bus: a horse-drawn, converted farm truck or conventional bus. Few students had cars and no mothers were running back and forth.

Alice and I would hit the back door at home about 4:30 with just one thought in mind. Food. It never occurred to us not to have a lunch when we got home. Usually bread and spread of some kind. But, as I look back upon it, Mother managed to have a pan of warm cinnamon rolls waiting for us more frequently

140

than she could afford to do considering the burdens of a home in those unmodern times.

Nothing ever tasted so good. We crammed them down. Then, ran to change clothes and start on the chores. It was a regular and unvarying routine. The chores are another story.

Change came much slower with schools than in many other facets of rural living. This 80-year-old one-room school, without electricity, was still in business in Mahaska County in 1949.

KINDS OF CHORES

Unvarying Ritual, Night and Morning

"DOING CHORES" had to be a litany when almost every farm family attempted to do a little of everything, raise a little of everything, and be as self-sufficient as possible. The idea of "store bought" bread, milk, butter, or canned goods was the kind of thing that only the most shiftless would be found doing.

Thus you had to have at the very least (and that was Dad's program; he didn't like to milk) one or two milk cows who needed attention night and morning every day of the year. If you were to be gone overnight for an extravagance like a day or two at the Iowa State Fair, the very least you had to do was get a neighbor to come in and "pail the old cows, water the chickens, and feed the dog and cats."

In addition to the milk cows and the chickens, we always had some hogs in various stages of the production cycle, a beef herd, some cattle on feed, usually a few sheep, and, of course, the horses. The routine changed greatly with the seasons, but during the school year it was the boy's job to hit the ground running when he got off the bus at 4:30 and go at a steady trot until suppertime. It was pretty much of a repeat in the morning, especially during spring and fall when the men were putting in all daylight hours in the field. Everything had to be fed and watered. There were always a few old sows or some calves in some pen or spot where it was necessary to carry water or wheel it there in a two-wheeled, homemade cart. There was just a lot of legwork; good jobs for a boy. Much had to be carried, both feed and water. Pens or stalls had to be cleaned out and bedded down, and a sharp eye kept at

143

all times to be sure that the accounted-for number of stock was on hand. When stock was running in the field or in pasture, I would jump on a horse, round them up, and head for the house. But woe unto me on those mornings when I had missed one or two which had been behind a hill when I rounded them. They would be at the gate wanting in, and when I saw that development I always tried to stay out of Dad's path for the rest of the chore period.

On one place we lived a dredge ditch ran through the far end of the farm and cattle would go there to drink. Sometimes they would mire down and not be able to get out of the mud. One time it was a couple of days before the absence of a cow brute was noticed; my fault.

To rescue a cow from that situation, we would drive back with the team and wagon, throw a long rope over the cow's head, hitch the other end of the rope to the back axle on the wagon, and say "giddap" to the team. The old cow's neck would stretch a good deal, but the body always came along with the head!

Doing chores was also the time to be sharp-eyed for nature's signs: any illness, the cow or calf or lamb that "didn't look just right," the sow that was "making her nest" and thus about ready to farrow, or being sure that mating processes were allowed to take place or prohibited depending upon your plan or the time of year.

When we had fat cattle in the yard, which we did rather regularly, Dad always looked after the feeding. He would hitch up a team to a wagon, night and morning, and drive out through the feedyard scooping the exact amount into the feed bunks as the cattle crowded around the team and the bunks. He counted the scoopfuls, increasing or decreasing the amount as his practiced eye dictated and throwing in just the right amount of supplement. It was not a job to be trusted to the hired man; he didn't know the "signs" which told whether to throw out three more or three less scoopfuls.

The last thing we would do at night, and the first thing we would do in the morning, would be the milking. You could do that after or before the outside chores. If we had two cows giving milk, both Dad and I would milk. The cats would gather around (we usually kept two or three as a result of a carefully controlled selection process) waiting for their breakfast or supper. They got a panful of warm milk as we finished the job; their meat diet was to be found around the crib or the granary. A boy and an old cat would soon learn the trick of having the boy direct a stream of milk—direct from the teat—halfway across the stall and the cat would "open wide" and take the offering direct. Naturally, it wasn't an exact science; the cat needed a bib. But it was a good game nevertheless.

The cows milked, the cats fed, Dad and/or I (the hired man looked after the horses; that was his job) would head for the house and supper. We would strain the milk into a can Mother would have standing on the back porch, wash, and be ready to eat. The chores were done. Except, if there were any farrowing, lambing, or calving prospects, we would be checking things out well into the night.

Don't they do chores on a farm any more? Not really. The horses are gone; farmers, like everyone else, have specialized. If they do chores they very likely have a lot to do and consider them a major part of the operation. Few farmers still "milk a few cows, keep a hundred old hens, and a few hogs."

Along about 4:30, when visiting somewhere on Sunday, our departure time would be routinely announced, "Well, about time to do chores." What do they say now?

Flies! You Wouldn't Believe It!

IN A MIDWESTERN SUMMER a fly trap at the back door was standard equipment! It was built of screen wire, circular, perhaps 12 inches across and 2½ feet tall. It stood up on legs an inch or so off the ground and the center of the bottom was cone-shaped—the cone pointing upward into the trap. A dish of sour milk beneath the trap would attract the flies and as they departed they moved up the cone and into the trap.

It was not uncommon to see a quart of dead flies in such a contraption, all victimized within a few feet of the back door. Such was fly population on the farm before the days of pesticides.

In spite of the trap the back screen door would be covered with flies. Dad would come in for a meal, wave his hat or jacket

145

to drive them away, and duck in the door. But not without followers. "Sticky paper," just like its name, perhaps 8 by 12 inches, was placed in strategic places throughout the house. Once touched by a wandering fly it held like epoxy.

But flies, a mere bother in the house, were an economic factor with livestock. Good farmers would use fly nets on their horses during the summer: nets with strings placed perhaps an inch apart, which were thrown over the horse, harness and all. As the horse moved, the nets moved and dislodged the flies.

Sometimes a herd of cattle would be seen to take off across the pasture on a dead run, tails in the air. The heel flies were after them. What there was about this particular fly, above all others, which brought this particular response, I never knew. The ultimate response to this fly sting was the starting of a cycle which ultimately caused a grub, the size of the last joint on your little finger, to develop in the animal and eventually work its way up through the back muscles and out through the hide. I used to squeeze these out of the back of my 4-H calves. What ultimate discomfort there was to the animal was not evident. But the flesh was damaged and the top hide, the best, was sharply reduced in value. Ultimately buyers "docked" cattle thus infested. Still do as a matter of fact. But pesticides have found their mark here, too.

Milking time, even with no more than the one or two cows standard with Dad, was never a pleasant time; none of us liked to milk. But milking time in the fly season was an especial burden. No self-respecting cow was happy to be stanchioned and have the flies given free reign over her carcass. She couldn't swing her head to dislodge those on her shoulders. But she could kick and she could, and did, switch her tail. Neither kicking nor tail switching was an exercise adding to the pleasure of a man (or boy) perched precariously on a one-legged stool at the bovine flank with a 12-quart pail clutched between his knees. Dad, on occasion, tied the old girl's tail to a handy post or upright. But this only further encouraged her leg action.

146

Butchering Was a Major Farm Event

BUTCHERING was a big event on the farm, and not only was there the excitement of it, but it was carefully planned to provide fresh meat as nearly as possible throughout the year and to meet the demands of peak farmwork. For instance, a hog would be butchered fairly late in the spring. Some of this meat could be used fresh to feed hired help and the rest cured or made into sausage. This combination was supposed to last until spring-hatched chickens were ready to go into the frying pan.

The chickens then went on into the fall and just as soon as the weather cooled down, another hog or two would be butchered. That was to look after the corn pickers. Later a beef would be butchered. Sometimes two would be butchered during the winter and we would divide each time with the Riches.

Butchering was a two-man-and-a-boy job. If it were a hog it took a lot of hot water. The big iron kettle was fired up first. Then a barrel was tipped up on a slant with its top resting against a platform built between a couple of sawhorses. This was all carefully arranged either under a tree from which to string the carcass or in front of a driveway in the corncrib where overhead beams took the place of a tree branch.

When the water was hot and a few handfuls of lye had been thrown into the kettle, the porker, rope attached to a hind leg, was herded out to the right spot and wrestled over on its back (no mean feat). The person most expert put a knife in exactly the right spot in the pig's neck. Whereupon the pig was let back on its feet while it rather promptly bled to death. The barrel was then filled with boiling water and the men hoisted the carcass up onto the platform. By immersing first the head end and then the rear end of the pig in the inclined barrel, they proceeded to "scald" the hog. This was not a sanitary measure; it was to loosen the hair. For unlike beef, the hide stayed on the pork carcass.

When the scalding process was finished, the men went after the carcass with a couple of scrapers and shortly the pig which might have been red, black, white, or a combination thereof, looked about as white and pink and clean as a freshly bathed baby!

Next a couple of slits were put in the rear hock joints, a singletree (what's that you ask?) was inserted to hold the legs far

147

apart and the hog, head down, was hoisted into the tree or over the crib beam with a block and tackle. At this point the carcass was opened from one end to the other and with a little careful work, to be sure that no offending guts were accidentally punctured to spew out over the meat, the carcass was soon devoid of entrails. The head was hacked off and tossed casually aside—to the dog's delight—and the guts heaved over into the hog yard where they were soon devoured and thus "recycled."

After the carcass had cooled, but before rigor mortis set in, Dad would take a meat saw and cut evenly through the backbone, dividing the carcass in half. Whereupon he would throw one-half over his shoulder and head for the house where it would be tossed down either on the kitchen table or on a table in the pantry.

Then began the "processing": trimming off the fat for lard, taking out the ham, shoulder, and bacon and the sausage material. Mother's work, of course, just began at this point.

On the old Hamilton place we had a smokehouse. It was about the size of a privy, but without the distinctive decoration in the door or the well-worn path. It was made of galvanized steel. The inside of the little building was dark and smelled strongly of smoke and cured pork. Hams, shoulders, and slabs of bacon would hang there much of the time. The smell was very distinctive and quite intriguing for a young boy!

Butchering a beef was different; no hot water, no scalding. But in other respects much the same. The steer or heifer, usually weighing 800 to 900 pounds, was one of the best in the feedyard. Dad and Mother didn't believe in feeding out "Choice to Prime" beef for market and then eating some "dairy calf" themselves.

The critter would be driven out of the feedlot, frequently lassoed and snubbed up to a post at the place where the butchering was to take place. Here a sharp lick with a sledge or an ax would stun the animal and a good big gash in the throat area would release a surprising volume of blood in great gushes. While this was going on, the block and tackle was raising the rear end of the carcass to assure complete bleeding. Then the hide had to be removed by skinning, a carefully done process as the hide itself was of some value. When stripped off it was covered with a thin layer of salt on the "meat" side and carefully rolled up and tied with twine. Eventually it would be sold to a hide merchant for a few dollars.

148

COURTESY *Wallaces Farmer*

*As soon as cool weather came in the fall, a hog or two
would be butchered to feed the corn pickers. Water for
scalding would be heated in an old iron kettle, poured
into a barrel, and the hog dumped in, first one end,
then the other, until the hair was ready to slip off.*

The carcass was strung up and again the gutting process took
place with care, with the entrails again dragged off to the hog
yard. (Hogs are both herbivorous and carnivorous; we had to be
careful to keep cows away from a hog yard at calving time; hogs
have been known to kill and eat a newborn calf. Also, to take
the place of proteins in a swine diet, I can recall some of our
more shiftless farmer neighbors who would buy an old pelter of
a horse, one headed for the rendering works, take it out in the
hog yard, shoot it, and leave the carcass for the hogs. They would
shortly reduce it to a stinking skeleton of bones, hide, and hoofs.)

Again the cooling-out process and the careful dividing of the
carcass took place. But with beef, the half had to be quartered
before Dad would toss it across his shoulder and head for the

149

kitchen or pantry. With beef, much more than with pork, there were the immediate "goodies"; not steaks and standing rib roasts, but liver, heart, and tongue. The liver at once, of course; the heart and tongue cooked and eaten either hot or in sandwiches.

Soapmaking: No Threat to the Soap Companies

Now, THE BIG OLD IRON KETTLES we used for butchering hogs and making soap are to be found in antique shops and go for a pretty penny. Few who buy them know of their original uses.

Soapmaking was Mother's job, with Alice and me helping.

150

When spring came, the accumulation of lard and fat from the various butcherings, plus bacon grease and the like, would be poured into the big kettle. Lye would be added and the mixture brought to a boil for the proper length of time. At a certain point in the cooling process, the many gallons of dark gray stuff with the consistency of syrup would be dipped out and put into low, flat containers of almost any kind. A flat box lined with cloth (to keep the hot soap from running out the cracks) was popular.

After the soap had hardened sufficiently, it was cut up into chunks perhaps the size of your fist and stored away in some place to cure for several months. When that process was complete the product was dark brown and about as hard as a store-bought cake of soap. To use it for laundry you took a knife and shaved off enough to bring the required suds. With the hard water so often used the amount required was considerable.

At other times the old kettle would be used to water some of the sheep running in the orchard. The water, of course, was carried two pailfuls at a time from the pump or tank.

Now, such kettles, which have seen many a pig converted to pork and boiled up many a gallon of soap, add the rustic touch to someone's split-level ranch home.

Death in the Barnyard Turns into Soap

PARTICULARLY in times of poverty, the ailment of an animal was taken almost as seriously as that of one of the family. The death of a horse or a cow was an especially serious thing.

When we lived south of Glidden we had the usual herd of purebred Angus cattle which we were pasturing on red clover. At that time we had much to learn about handling cattle under such conditions and we had some sad experiences.

The cattle, in the barnyard overnight, would be let into the pasture in the morning. They would fill up on clover wet with dew, and bloat. It was a frightening, and frequently deadly, thing. Gas would form in one of their several stomachs; in a matter of an hour or two at most their insides would fill to the

151

point of bursting. The hide would get tight as a drumhead; the bung would protrude; the eyes would stick out from the head. They would die promptly and horribly.

If you got there in time (there was no time to call the vet) the only solution was to take your jackknife, shut your eyes and puncture the belly. We lost several purebred cows that way and it was a bad financial blow at a time when things were on a fine balance.

A death like that would cast gloom over the whole family. Mealtime would be pretty silent. It was the financial loss, of course, but it was a personal thing, too. Perhaps the cow would have had a calf. In any case, each cow was known by both name and a number borne on a chain around her neck. This was for the purposes of purebred registry. It was a sad moment when Dad would take a screwdriver and remove the chain and number from the dead animal and turn his back on the carcass of what had been a valuable member of the barnyard family only hours before.

Another death that brought some wry amusement, although again a loss to the family, involved two old buck sheep.

Bucks always fight some; that is taken for granted. So if you had enough of a flock to require the attendance of two males, you looked for some regular sparring and a few good fights. The fights were a no-nonsense approach to the settlement of differences; the bucks simply backed off and came together on the dead run—head first. With no recourse to a remedy, one buck would get a splitting headache and the game was over. Sometime to keep the game from getting too rough the two sheep would be tied together with a reasonably short piece of rope. This kept them from getting far enough apart to really knock heads. Once Dad had just bought a new buck and, more or less to see the fun, turned him out with the flock which contained another buck. In no time at all the newcomer had been spotted, challenged, and battle lines drawn.

The two bucks whammed each other around at close range and then began to back off—farther and farther. Finally, as though some second had given the signal, they headed for each other at top speed.

With a great pop they met, head to head. One dropped as though he'd been shot. As it turned out, he might as well have been. Dad couldn't believe he was dead; just knocked out, he was sure. It was Sunday morning, I recall, and the duel had

152

taken place before breakfast. Dad was sure that "when we come back from breakfast he will be up and going." But he wasn't. It is a little hard to take the pulse of a sheep or use a stethoscope through a fleece. I remember we got Mother's hand mirror and held it up to the buck's nose. It didn't register.

A little shamefacedly and regretting also useless financial loss, we skinned the carcass and made soap out of the fat. Nice soap. But it smelled like sheep and so did all who used it. And it contributed nothing at all to the lamb crop.

Women's Lib in the Barnyard

THE PROTECTIVE INSTINCT of motherhood in farm animals is almost universal.

Reach under an old setting hen when she is on even just a nest of eggs, or particularly when she is hovering over a dozen chicks, and you will get a good sharp peck and she means business.

I have seen an old sow with a litter of pigs rear up and with loud and obviously angry vocal manifestations reach out and take hold of a human arm or leg. An old sow can be very mean.

Old ewes will not attack. But they will bat their eyes, stamp their feet, and particularly fend off a dog when it gets too close to a young lamb. (And with good cause, too; the bane of every sheep raiser is the dog or dogs which gets into a flock at night, runs them near to death, tears them up, and maybe kills a good many. It is an addictive sport with dogs and the only known cure is shooting.)

But old cows with calves are the most dangerous of all. At least ours were. As soon as calves came in the spring and until they were good-sized, I never meant to cross the cattle yard until I got big enough to carry a big stick and stand my ground. I had to get pretty good-sized before that was the case. A cow or cows with calves at side would put a dog over the fence on the dead run. With head up, nostrils wide, and eyes flashing, they would eye any intruder and, all of a sudden, charge. A full-grown man

153

they would not likely bother. But a boy or a dog, watch out!

At calf weaning time in the fall, it was time to put the calves in the feedyard and the cow back into the reproduction cycle. So the calves were locked in the barn and the cows in an outside lot or the pasture. For maybe three or four days, constantly, night and day but particularly at night, a steady, unvarying bellowing wail came from both calves and cows. The combined volume of twenty-five or thirty old cows and an equal number of offspring is substantial.

Three Typical Barnyard Operations

A COW BRUTE with horns can be a pretty ornery critter. Not so much with humans but with fellow critters. They soon drive all others away from the feed bunk and make life pretty miserable in the feedlot.

Our favorite old milk cow developed those tendencies. So one time when we were nipping off the horns of some young calves, Dad and Uncle Clyde (who helped on many two-man assignments) snubbed the old girl up to a post, took a saw and cut her horns off right down next to her head. There was a hollow place in the center of the horn and it seemed as though you could look right down into her brain, if any!

When they turned her loose she ran around the yard in a dazed condition, shaking her head as if in disbelief, with blood shooting out in little streams on both sides. For months after that there were bloodstains on the barns and gates and feed bunks. But shortly she healed up and the operation was considered a great success by the other cows who had felt her sharp horn in their ribs too often.

Bulls at a certain stage need a ring in their noses, the ring being a means of restraint and a pretty effective one. With a rope through the ring a man can pretty readily control a bull under most circumstances. With an ordinary halter the man might just as well shout "gee" and "haw" to a bull as to attempt to hold him in check.

So at a certain stage, when the bull calf was clearly destined

154

for parenthood rather than the feedyard, we would run him into a stanchion, tie his head, push the tine of a pitchfork through his nose, and insert the ring in the passage. It was fairly bloody little operation and not accomplished without a lot of kicking, bellering, and an occasional tearing up of a stanchion. Of course, had the bull only realized it, his options were that or another operation which he might have enjoyed even less.

Rooting pigs were a problem also. What makes a pig root, I don't know. With many now raised on concrete the problem is less acute than in the old days when hogs ran in the field until they were ready for market. But they would root around buildings, exposing foundations, and particularly under fences where they would make a hole and then disappear.

Curing that problem was a rainy day job. You "rung the pigs." The hired man, Dad, and I would run the pigs into the hog house and then as the hired man and I would grab a pig by the leg and drag him over to Dad, he would take a plier-like tool, crush a couple of "rings" into the foremost and obviously the tenderest part of the pig's snoot. As you might expect, the tendency to root was remarkably reduced.

Some Disagreeable Paternal Tendencies

WHILE THE OLD BUCK is a very protective animal, or at least, combative, he is also a kind of a coward. His primary approach is from the rear: a real sneak.

If you were less than alert and kid size, our old buck liked to find you off a distance of 20 or 30 feet, far enough to give him plenty of time to accelerate. That he would do and, head down and on a dead run, he would hit you square from behind. The result was obvious and a little terrifying although seldom fatal.

Dad always contended if you faced the buck he wouldn't hit you. But not too many had the courage to try. I remember Dad and a hired man were walking out across a sheep yard one time when the hired man, aware of impending attack, went by Dad like a shot as he shouted, "You face him; I'm going!"

We always kept a cowbell on the old buck so we could hear him coming. That was insurance but not total protection!

Chickens: For Eggs, Meat, and Bother

RAISING CHICKENS for both meat and eggs, regardless of the problems involved, was taken for granted. You needed 100 or maybe 200 hens plus an appropriate number of roosters. In the first place you ate a lot of eggs—for breakfast, of course. But also eggs kept better than meat during hot weather and thus scrambled eggs for supper was not uncommon. And if the "old hens were doing any good" you would accumulate a 12-dozen case of eggs by Saturday night which would be traded for staples.

By the Fourth of July, the young roosters would be about large enough (there was always about two weeks of debate on that subject before the first beheading) for frying. From then on until fall, there was just a lot of fried chicken.

To pick up a dinner on Sunday or any other day you took a pole with a wire hook on the end of it, a handful of corn, and headed for the backyard. You tossed out the corn and while the flock fought over the goodies, you slipped the hook over the leg of the largest looking rooster and he was on his way to the chopping block.

Of course, he had to be raised to that point. Farm raising of chickens went through three phases before it went out of business entirely.

First, in nature's way, a certain number of hens would get "broody" in the spring. They would refuse to leave the nest. The kids sent to hunt the eggs got a good sharp peck as they tried to reach under them. Those biddies were then ready to begin the incubation process.

You would get about fifteen eggs, put them in a straw-lined box over in a separate part of the hen house and put the old girl to work. She would settle down for a three weeks' stint, broken only by brief intervals, long enough to leave the nest to eat and drink from nearby supplies and to relieve herself irregularly but massively.

In due course she would bring off a brood. But the survival percentage would not be very great. Some eggs would be infertile; some chicks wouldn't survive the hatching process; others would fall prey to rodents and other barnyard hazards. Sometimes, in a rain, they would bunch up against a building in the worst possible place and drown. A few old hens would always "steal their nest

156

COURTESY *Wallaces Farmer*

out." That meant they had found a secluded spot, all of their own, in the haymow or under some trash.

At any rate, given the uncertainties of nature's way, a day came when, wonder of wonders, there was something called an incubator.

It was a flat box affair, mounted on legs bringing it up to table level and large enough to hold perhaps 200 eggs. We kept ours in a pantry just off the kitchen. When ready for business, it was fired up with some kind of jerry-built fuel oil arrangement. It demanded lots of attention for three weeks to keep the temperature constant. Also, it was necessary to "turn the eggs" at intervals, just as the old hen would do in the nest.

Something also had to take the place of the protecting wings of the old hen and the brooder house came into being. Here again it was weeks of care and concern to keep the temperature at just the right level. Too much heat led to respiratory ailments; too much cold caused the chicks to pile up and smother. Each year there would be news of an oil-warmed brooder house that caught fire and did away with the whole shebang.

The final chapter in the summer cycle of raising chickens, farm style, was getting the fool things to start living like civilized chickens in the hen house when fall came on.

As they grew up, and outgrew either their mother's protection or the brooder house, these young chickens reverted to nature and started roosting in trees or fences or most anywhere up off the ground.

157

As the days began to shorten and the first frost came into the air, it was time to round up the chickens. This was a family affair. Each armed himself with a broom, a rake, or a long pole, and at dusk, when the birds were just comfortably tucked into their illicit roosting spots, the family would start out through the grove and other roosting places, knocking chickens to the ground and attempting to shoo them in the direction of the open hen house door.

Chickens are dumb; "damn dumb," to quote Dad. And it was a pretty aimless and frustrating assignment to knock some half-asleep chicken off a branch and "suggest" it should figure out from that treatment that it should make a beeline for the hen house. Chickens ran in all directions. The family, poles, rakes, and brooms flailing, ran in all directions. Success, if it could be called that, was always something less than 100 percent. It usually took several nights to get all the stragglers. While the process was going on, there was always that nagging thought that confinement would mean that that fool hen house would have to be cleaned out later. Well, farmers finally quit raising chickens—for good reason!

And the Old Cow Coughed!

CATTLE ON GRASS, especially early in the spring, tend toward a certain looseness of the bowels, to put the matter plainly. The tail of the cow animal, being located where it is in relation to the elimination process, would sometimes get, shall we say, a little on the soggy side. Having that instrument wrapped around your neck during the milking process was not the type of experience which encouraged one to look with great favor upon the business of dairying. It was hot in the old unventilated barns when it came evening milking time. Thus if the old milk cow was reasonably cooperative we tended to try to crowd her up against the cow yard fence and milk outside. Once when Dad was following this procedure, or attempting to, he suffered an experience which made inside milking seem more attractive.

The cow in question, a little restless, tried to move away a

158

few steps at a time. That left Dad sitting there on the one-legged stool, pail clutched between knees, hands outstretched but sans cow or anything to hold in his hands. At one stage in this minuet, the cow stepped away, turned a bit, took aim and coughed. It was perfect timing. Dad was just leaning over to pick up the milk stool with one hand and had the milk pail in the other. His bib overalls gapped wide open. There was only one place for the reaction to that cough to go! Slowly he lowered the stool. And the milk pail! Carefully, continuing to lean over even though the trickle was already starting down each pant leg, he unbuckled the overalls, slid out of them with as much grace as the situation would allow, and made for the nearby stock tank. For obvious reasons. I was too scared to laugh—fortunately!

A Good Dog as Important as a Hired Man

OUR DOG (only one at a time) and a limited number of cats were always at our back door. Today there are reported to be 10,000 brands of pet food available, but the idea of store-bought food for them then was as remote as it would have been to have bought milk for the family. It just wasn't done.

Contrary to one of the no-nos in the suburban pet world today, "No chicken bones; they may puncture something," our dogs lived on chicken bones. Chicken was the Hamilton family's main diet from about the Fourth of July until cold weather made it possible to butcher a hog. After the meal a great mound of bones would end up in the dog dish or else just in a heap in the backyard. The dog loved them; his mealtime sounded like a modern disposal at work—which it was—and if the bones ever punctured anything he kept it strictly to himself. He was lucky, I guess, for such things can be fatal.

Dogs and cats were pets at our house, very much so, but they were also utilitarian. A family who kept a bunch of "worthless dogs" around the back door was looked upon with disdain. Dad practiced zero population growth with cats before the phrase had ever been heard of.

159

The dogs, Jimmie, Gyp, Carlo, were all collies. Unlike horses, bought young and frequently sold off before they had used up their usefulness, dogs were kept from puppyhood until old age or accident claimed them. They were carefully trained, well disciplined, and of great help in handling stock.

One steer or hog or old ewe could break out of a herd and quickly outrun any man or boy in sight. But old Jimmie, with hardly a word, would race out and head them back into the flock or herd in no time. A bunch of sheep would start milling; shouting, clubbing, whistling were of no avail. But a dog would start them in forward motion in short order. Or the cattle would be spread out all over the pasture. Dad would whistle to the dog, point out in the general area of the stock, and Jimmie would lope out around the most remote critter and start them all moving toward the barn. Never running them; not too fast. But always moving them. If he forgot one, Dad would whistle and point out the oversight and Jimmie would correct the error.

Well-trained dogs are intelligent creatures and very useful on a general stock farm. Of course, as pups they had to be trained. Chewing up overshoes and ordinary stuff like that were not the problems; it was sucking eggs. For some reason a young pup is much attracted to a warm, freshly laid egg. Once they have tasted one, they quickly become an "eggomaniac"; the habit is addictive.

We would watch the new pup like the proverbial hawk, but just like the problem drinker, he would escape our sight and soon we would find nothing but some slimy remains in the hen's nest where he had gobbled up one egg after another. We tried to cure it by puncturing an egg, filling it with pepper or some equally hot substance, with a "that-will-teach-him" idea. I never remember it working. But we finally cured it some way.

We never had a cross dog, but they were always very protective of my sister and me when we were youngsters. They were never kept in the house, or even let in the house. They were never tied. In the winter they slept in the barn; in the summer they had their own little spot around the back door. They were up and ready to get the cows from the pasture or the stalk field as soon as anyone stirred in the morning. They were the last animal you spoke to at night. And if the cattle should break down a gate or get through the fence at 2 A.M. they sounded the alarm and were on the job.

Our dogs were not pets; they were simply members of the

160

family, working members. They didn't get shots. They didn't get distemper. And none ever suffered the typical fate of the town dogs, getting run over by a car. One of our favorites, a beautiful big white collie, did get run over by a train. When he didn't come home, we knew something was wrong and Dad found the remains along the right-of-way.

I have heard Dad say, and he wasn't given to rhetoric, that his dog was worth as much as a good hired man!

I said never a cross dog. One time we were butchering. Dad and the hired man had just finished the process and a carcass was hanging up in the shed to cool. A neighbor dropped by and said in the kind of kidding, jocular way that might be expected:

"Well, I am glad to see where your meat is hanging; I will know where to stop by and get some tonight."

Whereupon the dog, who had been standing in the circle, reached up and took a firm hold on the neighbor's hand.

It was the only time he had ever been known to touch a person and why remained a mystery—to all except the hired man. He was always sure that that dog fully understood what was being said. That act confirmed his belief.

Our two or three cats, well, they were important and we took pains to feed them warm milk night and morning. Some of them were great pets and sometimes they did get in the house, for a short period. But their rank order in the scheme of things was far, far below that of a dog. They could catch mice, and were supposed to, but, after all, they could hardly be expected to go and round up the cows!

Manure: Well, There's a Lot of Difference

BEFORE THE DAYS of chemicals, the cycle of crops to livestock and the "end product" back to the soil was more important than it is now. The difference in crop yields between the livestock farmer

161

and the strictly grain farmer was pretty pronounced. The problem was to get the fertilizer from barnyard to field. Just as corn picking was an ear at a time, getting the manure back to the field was a forkful at a time. Our manure spreader was pulled by three horses. Once loaded you headed for the field. There the moving apron was activated and as the load pushed back against the beater-spreader it was discharged in a kind of eggbeater effect. If by chance you happened to be going with the wind, the driver might be pretty well pelted.

Loading the spreader was just a long, slow job. If you were taking the pile which had been accumulating outside the back barn door where it had been heaved a forkful at a time during the winter, either from behind the milk cows or the horses, it was just a tedious, smelly job. If the manure were in the cattle shed, where it had been tramped and added to a layer at a time all winter long, with a fresh layer of bedding added at regular intervals, the texture was about the same as (excuse the comparison) chewing tobacco. It was tough, heavy, and compacted. You pushed a four-tine manure fork into the substance, perhaps 8 or 10 inches deep, and eventually worked loose a forkful. Perhaps you couldn't get into the shed with the spreader and so you walked a half-dozen steps and tossed the forkful through the door into the waiting spreader, its horses switching flies as they waited for the process to be completed.

But loading and spreading cattle and horse manure was as nothing compared to the hen house job. Cleaning the hen house was a job universally detested by hired men, boys, and bosses alike. After the chickens had been confined in the house all winter the roosts were many inches deep with the results. Hen houses were always, it seemed, a low, cramped, lean-to type of structure, half of which was taken up with a platform about 4 feet off the ground. Roosts, long poles or 2 x 2 boards, were laid across this platform in rows about a foot apart and raised perhaps 6 inches off the platform. At the first sign of early darkness the flock, with some clucking and bickering, would fly up to these roosts and arrange themselves, row on row, to spend the next twelve to fourteen hours in a semimoribund state. But their bowels kept moving!

By spring the roosts were many inches deep. The job was evident. The unlucky person pulled the spreader up to the hen house door, got up on the roosts in a semicrouched position, removed the roosts, and with fork, shovel, and broom began to remove what the chickens had left behind. There is a minimum of moisture in poultry droppings, particularly after some months, and the job was dusty, dirty, and miserable. (Here again I am reminded, as with carrying cobs for the stove, that Mother sometimes undertook this hen house job when all the men were "just too busy"!)

And then there was the hog house. Compared to the hen house, cleaning up after hogs was a joy—except for one thing: odor. To this very day, scientists and chemists have not been able to alter feed intake or in any other way change the end result of a hog operation so that its odor does not penetrate and cling to humans, their clothing, and all else that comes in contact with the product.

The nighttime habits of hogs are most fastidious. Throw a good bed of any dry material into a hog shed and come back three days later. Ninety-five percent of it will be clean and dry. The hogs will have decided that one corner is their bathroom and all of their elimination will be deposited within a well-circumscribed area. Pigs may "eat dirty" but they like to sleep dry and warm. They do not wet the bed.

Then there is horse manure—a totally different product.

Our horses would be kept two in a stall, tied to the manger containing a feed box and hay bunk. In the morning, you asked Laura to step first to one side and then the other while you tidied up her bed and put in fresh bedding.

This product was carried to the back door or a waiting window and given a heave. In a month's time a dozen head of horses would provide a fair little heap where again the manure loading and spreader-to-the-field operation took over.

Before the days of electric tank heaters, horse manure had a characteristic of special value around the farm in the winter. It "heats." The chemistry of a pile of horse manure is such that in the coldest day of the winter, it gives off a good little pillar of steam. A pile of horse manure doesn't freeze and snow on it constantly melts. In short, there is energy there to be put to work. In the days before electricity or bottled gas this heat-giving energy had to be put to use. It could be used to "bank" the foundations of a hog house or hen house and thus reduce the drafts that otherwise made those buildings as cold or colder than out-of-doors. Occasionally, a less fastidious farm family had been known to use that same material to bank the foundation of the house itself, the family's house that is. But it was pretty aromatic for that use; generally, bales of straw were used.

The primary use to which this useful characteristic of horse manure was put was in keeping stock watering tanks from freezing solid. A "Cowboy" tank heater was a kind of submersible gadget that was weighted down in the stock tank. Into one end were fed cobs and wood and out the other end came the smoke.

164

But its effectiveness was of short duration; the fire quickly went out. So when fall came a major get-ready-for-winter task was to build a cover over the stock tank, solid except for a couple of tight-fitting doors. Then the whole thing, except for these small doors, was covered with 2 or 3 feet of horse manure. The "heating" process began and if the covers were kept closed except for brief periods when the stock was drinking, your freeze-up problems for the winter were over.

Occasionally, a good soaking rain in the fall or in spring before the cover was removed would color the water in the tank to a not exactly "ocean blue." But the stock didn't seem to mind.

A load of manure went off easier than it went on.

"Worst Damned Calf I've Ever Seen"

DAIRYING wasn't Dad's thing. We usually kept two old milk cows with the idea that at least one of them was fresh at all times; part of the year they would both be giving milk and we usually had at least one or two pails of milk both night and morning. When Dad and I would come in with the milk, Mother would have a fresh, clean pail sitting out on the porch. We poured the milk through a strainer and that was as close as the product ever came to pasteurization. "Foreign material" in the milk pail was not unknown! But it was good clean dirt and the cows were always tuberculosis tested.

(I speak casually here of having our cows tuberculosis tested. When it became the law of the land—along in the twenties—that all bovines had to be so tested the idea was heatedly, and violently, rejected by some farmers. Government veterinarians, armed with orders to test a herd, were driven off farms at gunpoint. That led to the "cow war" in southeast Iowa. But that's another story.)

Once strained the warm milk was placed, during the summer, in the coolest place available. This might be in the well sump or in the basement. Neither place was very cool. Then the cream would rise and Mother would skim this off with a big ladle-like skimmer. The cream would be so thick and heavy the whole top of the pail would come off in one piece, like the scum on a paint pail left too long uncovered. As a matter of fact the cream, once in the cream pitcher on the table, would be so thick we would spoon it out onto our cereal!

Cholesterol? A word yet unknown at least on the farm. As if it weren't enough to clog your arteries with what you could pile onto your cereal, Mother would pour some more in the chicken gravy! But what was a little butterfat when eggs and

This man has milked by hand, no doubt in some hot, unventilated barn, his head up against the cow's flank and the sweat trickling down his belly. The whole purpose of milking and "separating" is that tiny, tiny stream of butterfat going into the cream can. By repeating that sequence twice each day for a week, the farmer collected a few gallons of very sour cream which he sold for a few dollars or traded for a few groceries.

166

good, fat bacon were standard fare for breakfast and a big plate of scrambled eggs would take the place of meat for supper during the summer when refrigeration was a problem. Eggs provided their own keeping qualities, at least for limited periods.

With the cream removed, the rest of that pail of milk was poured into a big pitcher which always sat by Dad's place. Two or three glasses of milk for each member of the family at each meal were about par.

Other milk would be simmering on the back of the stove for cottage cheese (always served with sugar syrup) and the cream that we didn't eat was poured into a can where it soured naturally. At a certain stage of sourness it was ready for churning, a tedious job done with a dasher churn. The problem was getting the raw material chilled down to the proper temperature. I remember many a time when we took turns on the churn handle and it seemed as though the butter would never "come." Sometimes it didn't; we gave up in despair. When it did the butterfat would begin to congeal in first small and then bigger and bigger lumps and finally they could be scooped out into a wooden bowl, salted, and worked into a mold of a couple pounds or so. This with a wooden butter paddle. Left over in the churn, of course, was thick, rich buttermilk still carrying a few small chunks of butter. A glassful, salted, was a tangy, refreshing drink and one of real substance. The last guy on the churn usually had a glassful. But it was generally a leftover product for the chickens. It was too acid and sour for the cats and dogs.

Sometimes we had more cream than we needed for making butter and the extra was saved during the week and taken to town on Saturday night, where it was traded for groceries. We would have only a gallon or two of our product, and that, along with that of many neighbors, would be poured into larger cans in the back of the general store, after it was tested for butterfat, and eventually hauled off to some creamery for conversion to butter.

That process, and the kind of butter that resulted, contributed to the growth of vegetable spreads—for obvious reasons! But I have left out one step. In order for the cow to give milk she had to freshen—to have a calf. What to do with the calf when you wanted the milk?

Well, as soon as nature had provided the calf what only its mother could provide in those first few days after birth, you put the calf in a nearby pen, milked the mother, and taught the calf

168

to drink out of a bucket. Of course, you fed him skimmed milk; no use wasting butterfat on a dairy calf.

The problem was teaching the calf to drink. It came into the world knowing about nursing but there was nothing in the genes that said anything about buckets. So we would teach him to be a "bucket calf." Dad would get a bucket of milk and crowd the calf back into a corner of the pen. He would then get one arm around the calf's neck while holding the milk bucket in the other hand. Finally, the calf would have his rear squarely back in the corner and Dad would swing a leg over his neck (still talking about the calf—although before this operation was over Dad might have his leg over his own neck)! The next step was to push the calf's head into the bucket which hopefully still contained some milk. But the calf doesn't know about drinking; he's a sucker. So you forced his nose down into the milk, reached down and slipped your middle finger up into his mouth. The idea is for the calf to suck the finger and in the process absorb enough milk—with his nose clearly below the "water line"—so that you can slip your finger out and lo, he is a "bucket calf."

That's the idea. But what really happens? Many things. First option is for calf to lunge forward, upsetting Dad and spilling the milk bucket. That is Very Bad; the calf will get a swift kick and not very polite words. Second option: the calf's nose is well below the water line and just before drowning begins he snorts. Better part of milk goes up Dad's sleeves and all over his face. That is not good but not as bad as option one.

After four or five days of action involving Option One or Option Two or numerous interesting variations, plus many unkind words on Dad's part, he swears this is the "Worst damned calf I have ever seen."

The alternative being starvation, the calf finally learns to drink out of a bucket. And then the reverse sets in. The very sight of a bucket of milk sends the calf into a near spasm of excitement. With a pail of milk in your hand, you can't get in the pen with him without his practically taking you down in his excitement to get his head in the bucket. In the process he is very likely to butt the pail around and spill half of it in your shoe. After a few great inhalations, he seems to be quieting down and you leave him to finish the pail. Whereupon he is again overtaken with excitement and spills whatever is left. And Dad says, "Worst damned calf I have ever seen."

169

PART EIGHT DANGERS,

A COMMON PART OF LIFE

Close Calls

MODERN FARM MACHINERY sometimes overturns and kills. Gears sometimes grab fingers, arms, and legs and leave bloody stumps.

But farming in the good old days was not without its dangers too. Hazards with livestock could be serious. I remember the story of Dad coming to the house with deep welts and cuts in his back. An old cow with a new calf had taken exception to his presence, knocked him down, and trampled him. People were seriously hurt in runaways. The list could go on.

I remember two scary accidents that happened when working with Dad and our chores.

We had a black-snake whip, 6 or 8 feet long. I loved to make it snap. One day I was practicing in a stall in the barn. It flicked into the next stall and caught Old Buck across the rear hocks. With that she lashed out, kicking as hard as she could with both feet straight out.

Dad was unharnessing her at that time and had just turned his back to hang the harness on the wall. Three inches more and she would have hit him square in the middle of the back—and broken it most certainly!

Another time we were attempting to close a haymow door. It was dark and threatening to storm. Dad and I were pulling the carrier out to the end of the track with the idea that it would release (as it properly should have) the fork mechanism. But the operation malfunctioned and the whole unit came sailing off the end of the track—30 feet or so in the air—and directly at us. It couldn't have weighed less than 20 pounds. It was semidark and

171

we looked up just in time to duck. It could easily have killed us.

The time my dear little King spooked, just as I went to mount him, and I was thrown across the saddle, the tiniest slip would have tossed me off and if a foot had caught in the stirrup there is no doubt I would have been a statistic within a matter of minutes. More than one person has been dragged to death under such circumstances.

Swimming pools were unknown in the olden days. Thus ponds and gravel pits were favorite and obviously dangerous places for dipping. Furthermore the opportunities to learn to swim were slim. I didn't learn until forced to as a college freshman.

But still there was the temptation to visit the gravel pits. The boys in town had more time to practice than I did and so I was always at a disadvantage when we ended up in such circumstances.

At a pit near Lanesboro we were splashing around when I panicked. Suddenly there was nothing under my feet. Forest (Snooky) Thorne reached out, grabbed my hair, and pulled me into shallow water. Otherwise, another statistic.

From Scarlet Fever to Salk!

QUARANTINE—SCARLET FEVER——QUARANTINE—SMALLPOX

Signs like those for communicable diseases were a commonplace means of warning: stay away! They were big and rather threatening, with type large enough to be read at some distance and tacked right by the front door. In town, at least, they were put up by police. Remind you of stories of the plague? They were red and yellow in color, very bold. Over the years their use tended to decline. However, as recently as 1950, under the heading of "placarding," the Iowa State Department of Health Rules and Regulations Concerning the Control of Communicable Diseases was still presenting the advantages of "posting warning notices." The department's handbook explained where placards were available and also spelled out the ground rules under which "The breadwinner may be allowed to live in the house [where a communicable disease is present] and attend to his work" . . .

172

under certain conditions. But it finally said to forget the placards.

But I remember Dad telling of being quarantined with scarlet fever under what apparently were fairly typical circumstances. He was confined to an upstairs room in which a stove had been installed in some way. The family brought him fuel and food and carried out the slop jar each day.

In many cases, particularly with small pox and diphtheria, everything in such a room would be burned when the siege was over. But that was not sufficient. The house itself would be fumigated. This meant sealing the house and burning something that would create a gaseous disinfectant such as formaldehyde or sulphur. Later it was proven that this made the house smell better, if you liked the smell of formaldehyde or sulphur, but was totally ineffective for the purpose intended.

Naturally a kid confined to a room under such circumstances got another disease, something called cabin fever. Ruth recalls a neighbor boy so incarcerated. He had an early-age interest in a girl and Ruth used to pass notes to him on a rope he would drop out the window for such messages. Her mother was sure that she would "get something" via rope transmission.

These diseases, before the days of inoculation, were, of course, serious indeed. Elsewhere in this recital are the reports of children dying two and three at a time from such ailments.

But some other kid diseases were of a less serious nature. For example, ringworm and "the itch." Ringworm, "the itch" (not to be confused with just plain "itch"), and athlete's foot have a good deal in common; if you have had one you can sympathize with anyone afflicted with the other.

I had ringworm a few times. Ringworm was common on the calves I was raising and the first thing we knew, a small red spot on my hands, neck, or in my hair had erupted and enlarged into a gooey, scaly, itchy mess. My worst case got started around an ear, quickly spread into my hair, and turned the ear itself into a typical wrestler's cauliflower job but one that dripped and scaled and itched. I went around school one winter with a wide bandage around my head and was dubbed "Pete the Sheik"—Pete being a nickname that naturally enough came from Old Pete, the horse I sometimes rode.

There were gradations of social status associated with these ailments. For example, anyone could get ringworm, but "the itch," whether properly or not, was identified with those who were not frequently enough exposed to soap and water. You avoided them for that reason as well as fear of "the itch."

"The itch," incidentally, is officially recognized in medical terminology as scabies and it is known to be spread by "the itch mite" which burrows under the skin.

Closely related to "the itch," although not scientifically, were lice. The word would get around that some kids had lice. Whether true or not was probably not known for sure by any except the kids themselves. But those cruelest of all human beings, kids, never bothered to doubt. So-and-so "has lice"! Stay away from him!

Soldiers had lice in World War I, for lack of ability to wash and change clothes, and they were called "cooties." The lice, that is, not the soldiers! Kids loved that name. Let some kid begin to dig an armpit or his crotch and the cry would ring out: "Cooties, cooties, Joe's got the cooties!" Joe was thus destroyed—socially.

In the same general order of things were bedbugs. These tiny little creatures set up housekeeping in cracks in old floors, in old loose plaster walls, and particularly in beds and mattresses. They came out of all these places at bedtime, attached themselves to the victim, and settled down for a long blood-sucking night. Places to be suspicious of were cheap hotels, rooming houses, and anyplace where concern for sanitation was not excessive.

Dad used to be concerned as he rode into Chicago with cattle in the old "cattlemen's cars" which were attached to the livestock trains. These old day coaches had had plenty of opportunity to accumulate almost all the diseases or discomforts known to human beings.

Most of these pests and ailments began to depart with the horse and buggy. But it was soap and running water that did them in, not the Model T.

More than sanitation, however, was needed for other ailments; for instance, the flu epidemic of 1918–1919. The world was at war but the flu epidemic that spread around the world killed more than 20 million people, far more than were felled by bullets. It swept through the barracks, of course, but it likewise raced across the countryside through the towns and cities.

Ruth recalls that in her parents' circle of friends in Blair, "It seemed as though half their friends died of flu in one winter."

Flu caused panics in communities. But, unbelievable as it is now, in what seems to many of us no time at all, polio did the

174

same thing. Salk vaccine came only in the middle fifties.

I was running the newspaper in Iowa Falls when one of the last pre-Salk outbreaks of polio hit that community. An "outbreak" was three or four cases at any one time. Such an outbreak would strike fear and terror into any family with children where the mother and father saw each sniffle or complaint as only weeks away from that awful basket-case paralysis situation. Sometimes it happened. Perhaps it was only a weakened leg to be corrected with a brace. You still see such braces today on persons thirty years or older. Polio might also totally paralyze the victim, confining him or her to life in an iron lung. Or, perhaps he would be able to breath and swallow but no other bodily functions would remain operative. Such victims are now largely forgotten; you can see the basis for a parent's concern.

In the Iowa Falls outbreak public gatherings were suspended. Children were confined to their own yards. Farm people quit coming to Iowa Falls to shop. Business dried up on Main Street. Rumors were rampant as to (1) numbers stricken, and (2) possible causes. Everyone had his theory and medical or scientific advice was ignored. The word would go around that the outbreak stemmed from the fact that Ross Comly was keeping horses within city limits. At the other extreme came "the word" that the disease was spread through the eating of bananas!

The youthful victims were rushed by ambulance to Des Moines hospitals. The last thing that we did before going to press every Tuesday and Thursday morning was to call the families or the hospitals and get a report as complete and nearly accurate as possible. Although only a few inches in length, it was the biggest news in the paper.

Businessmen called to discourage continued reporting. The folks in Radcliffe and other small communities, they said, were afraid to come to town. That was bad for business.

I maintained that if we told the people in Radcliffe about what was happening when the outbreak was going on they would believe us when we said good health had returned. This elementary fact was lost on some of my business friends. It didn't do anyone's business any good, mine or theirs.

With inoculations, antibiotics, running water, and Salk, have we seen the last of epidemics and outbreaks?

A Pig and a Boy Each Get Shot

MOST FARM KIDS carried a gun. How so many of them grew up is a bit of a mystery. How their mothers survived I don't know. I had a .22 caliber rifle under my arm hours at a time long before I was big enough to do fieldwork and then the rifle was standard equipment evenings or weekends.

It was the same with other boys and also when we were together, just "messing around," on Sundays. Squirrels, birds, tin cans, fence posts, rabbits, everything got some attention.

I remember one time when Mother was slicing some bacon from a home-butchered hog and cut right by a .22 slug imbedded in the porker's side. We were all right there when it happened and I remember Dad suggesting, just a little dryly, that "it wouldn't hurt anything to be a little more careful with that gun." That was all.

One Sunday a bunch of us boys were skating on a dredge ditch which ran along the back of our farm. One of the boys had a .410 shotgun, the lightest thing going in shotguns.

I was skating a little ways away from the group when the gun went off and I instantly felt a stab in the back. I was scared and let out a yell. The others were equally frightened and came scrambling to where I was. We had all been warned repeatedly. All had taken the oath to be careful. Yet here was one of us shot in the back!

I began to peel off the layers of coats, sweaters, shirts, and underwear, anticipating each would be blood-soaked—and wondering how I could get from that remote corner of the farm to the house and presumably to a doctor.

Finally the peeling off process was completed. Sure enough, I had been shot with just one pellet (why one pellet we never could figure out) from that .410. There was just a nice little red welt where I was certain a bloody wound would be found. But the scare was for real. So far as I know, the shot in my back and in that pig were the only shots that went astray. So far as I know!

176

Whooping Cough Has Its Rewards—for Pigs

ONE OF THE CHILDHOOD AILMENTS—whooping cough—came late to Dad. This overtook him one winter along in middle age. We kids were vaccinated. He was the only one of the family that succumbed.

Whooping cough didn't get him down; it isn't, or wasn't, that kind of an ailment.

But cough he did! You could hear him even when he was clear down in the barn. But his worst spells would overtake him when he left the house and took the first breath of cold air.

The winter he suffered from this kid disease we raised a bunch of fall pigs and they ran loose in the barnyard.

Every once in a while Dad's cough would get the best of him, just as he was leaving the house after a meal, and he would double over and upchuck the bread and gravy.

In no time at all these young pigs learned that the sound of Dad's cough might well be the signal for a free lunch. And so with the first mighty hack, pigs would come running in all directions, gathering around Dad like so many puppy dogs, and showing all kinds of disappointment if the anticipated results were not forthcoming. Dad didn't think it was so very funny! But the neighbors thought it was uproarious!

Getting Buried Was a Two-Step Process

CAME THAT INEVITABLE TIME in the life cycle when it was necessary to do two things for friends or relatives: "lay out the body," and "sit up with the corpse."

"Laying out the body" was no doubt more widely practiced in rural areas than in town. But Mother recalls that her father was called on many occasions, after they moved to the river farm northeast of Glidden, to "come in and lay out the body." This "honor"—if it could be so considered—was reserved for one of the more respected members of the community. Mother recalls that Granddad would sometimes observe that certain neighbors might not pay him much heed until death occurred and then they would call: "Mr. Heaton, will you please come in and lay out Uncle Jed." Not too much information available on what was involved in laying out Uncle Jed. It wasn't embalming!

To whatever extent there was anything like a doctor or coroner to make things official seems a little vague. Apparently the family could figure death out for themselves. As well they might. For with such medical attention as there was available only by horseback or horse and buggy, and before the days of vaccination, death struck quickly and often repeatedly.

Ella Stotser, whose grandparents were among the early settlers in Hardin County, told me of the time her grandparents went into a neighboring home struck down with diphtheria. It was winter and at one time the bodies of three small children were laid out on the porch together!

Early burials also tended to be somewhat less "structured" than those now prevailing.

My father told of the hired man working for a neighbor who lived "back in the woods." The hired man plowed a certain area near the orchard whereupon the observation was offered, "I'm sorry we forgot to tell you; that's where the graves are. But then I guess they would have been plowed over sometime anyway."

During that interlude between the "laying out process" and burial it was necessary to "sit up with the corpse." This custom hung on for some time. Ruth remembers the friends and neighbors "sitting up" when her Grandfather Farnham died in 1925. The sitting up took place in the parlor where the bodies remained prior to the funeral.

In the earliest period of Mother's recollections, embalming was not a customary practice in certain rural areas at least. She recalls that they covered the bodies with clothes dipped in some kind of fluid—for preservative purposes. "But they still had the funerals pretty promptly."

Later the body, although it might be returned to the family parlor, would be carted off by the local furniture dealer for embalming. Undertaking and the furniture business seemed to go hand in hand—in a clammy sort of way. The furniture dealer had the equipment: caskets. All he had to do was learn the funeral techniques.

The furniture man, not finding a display of caskets a real door buster in attracting business, kept the undertaking part of

178

his operation in the back room. At an earlier time he showed a fine sensitivity for the situation by always keeping a matched team of black horses to haul the hearse.

Funerals were frequently held in the home. Neighbors would bring in chairs; some would stand. The family would stay upstairs but with the door open so they could hear the services.

On the first call, as the furniture dealer–undertaker came to get the body, he would bring a wreath done up with a black ribbon. This would be attached to the front door until after burial. Taking down the wreath was a last gentle goodbye.

As with many facets of life today, affluence and things material—funeral homes, floral displays, paid musicians—have taken from death much of the simple dignity which accompanied that event when it was more nearly a family and friends affair.

The drouth of 1936.

AFTERWORD

IT HAS BEEN SAID that at times a person of very ordinary wit can hardly avoid success, while contrarily, in other times and circumstances, a person of uncommon ability cannot escape defeat. Many of those active in farming between the two wars fell in this latter category.

From the "slump in farm prices" after World War I until World War II there were no "good times" in agriculture; they were generally very bad. FDR and the New Deal turned things around but only to the extent that farmers could "hang on" where they had been going through the foreclosure route before.

Against that generally unhappy backdrop for agriculture, which felt none of the heady experiences of Wall Street that led to "the crash," came the worst depression of this century.

How did farmers react to 10-cent corn, 3-cent hogs, loss of farms, foreclosures—to hard times?

In various ways, of course, but many, most, reacted as my parents did. Depressions and hard times had been before—in the 1890s; they would come again. They were something to be borne—with dignity and without undue complaint.

Work hard. Save. Be honest. Mother would observe that our clothes might be patched, but they would be clean.

Yes, there was agitation for "farm relief" all during the twenties. But that was not new. The Populists and the Grangers had been fighting the "eastern interests" almost from the beginning. So during the twenties and early thirties there came the McNary-Haugen Bill and the Federal Farm Board.

But many felt that government "tinkering" would be only a palliative and eventually the solution (what solution?) would come through sweat and frugality. Burt Hamilton was one who felt thus. It was his contention that "we have to let this thing go through the wringer and start over."

Not all felt that way.

As close as two counties to the west of us, in western Iowa, there were "penny auctions." At a sheriff's sale neighbors would bid pennies for the various items and return the item to the original owner. The response of the sullen crowd, some armed with pitchforks and axe handles, quickly gave the word to anyone not playing the game.

At LeMars, in northwest Iowa, a judge who refused to halt the wheels of justice which would have ended in foreclosure, was dragged from his bench, hauled to the country, a rope put around his neck and his life threatened. Such incidents are recorded elsewhere so we need not elaborate.

But, to a large degree, conservative, Republican-voting midwestern farmers accepted hard times as pretty much inevitable: work hard and save! By 1932, however, they had had enough. They were ready to vote for Franklin Roosevelt.

The New Deal brought startling new concepts to the previously accepted relationships between government and people. On the farms there were commodity loans, farmers actually being paid for holding acres out of production; low-interest loans for tenants seeking ownership; rural electrification; payments for soil conservation practices; farmers elected to committees who, clear down to the township level, spoke for the federal government! Breathtaking!

All those forces were having great impact when came Hitler and World War II. To win that war, the United States took its economy to pieces and put it together all over again. It was all different. Forced-draft technology developed to win the war was upon the land. As millions of young Americans from farms, hamlets, towns, and cities went off to fight together in areas all around the world, they came back to their communities different persons than when they left.

It all changed—in no time at all!

How did my parents, who have appeared in earlier parts of this effort, how did they—on a one-to-one basis—face these difficult and rapidly changing times?

In what should have been their most productive years they were losing a farm and "starting over." But this was no time for cynicism, or bitterness, or railing at Washington, or complaint. You didn't question "the system." You had made a mistake. Start over.

Of course it wasn't just losing a farm. For when you are "down" minor misfortunes become major and one thing seems to lead to another. We were just about hailed out one June day in the early thirties. Then there was the drought of 1936, the like of which has not been repeated since. Day after day of searing temperatures and hot, southwest winds. The corn would

182

"roll" and fire. Chickens would seek the shade and flop down, wings extended, beaks gaping open. All living things sought shade. There would be lightning at night and new hope. But it was heat lightning! Each day and each hour of the day you would scan the skies for clouds. They didn't come and at breakfast someone would predict "another scorcher." He was right.

Spirits were as low as the temperatures were high as crops withered relentlessly away, day after day.

Then there were the dust storms. These were not those of the Plains. But psychologically (and financially, too, for that matter) they were a depressing time. Fence rows and ditches drifted full. Corn 3 and 4 inches high would be cut off at the ground by blowing silt. The sky would darken and cars would drive with their lights on. Everything you ate, touched, or wore felt gritty, even the sheets on your bed. It was not just a good thick layer of dust throughout every room in the house and in every cupboard and closet; there would be drifts of dirt around every loose-fitting door and window. And they all fit loose!

Too, there was a general neglect of dental and medical care. There was the cost; you went to the dentist when you had a toothache, not for preventive dentistry. Both my parents had a full set of dentures while I was still in the grades and high school.

Dad's stomach "bothered him"; he had an ulcer. I have seen him have rheumatism so badly he would use the pitchfork to pick up a milk stool and then in utter agony sit down to milk. But he was doing fieldwork all the time, maybe walking all day behind a four-horse team.

A generation or two earlier, "breaking the Plains broke many women." Mother's health was remarkably good. But she could not have helped being right out at the edge many times.

I emphasize that these same general circumstances were shaping the atmosphere of most farm homes of the time in question.

What did it do to the people? Well, of course sunny days restored some bounce. And various people carry burdens in different ways.

In the case of my parents, to speak more personally, it was my Mother who was the strong one in many respects. Complaints from her were virtually unknown. Even in her "down" moments she was worried about others who might be suffering more. No matter how badly she might be hurting inside, her outward

183

demeanor was almost unvarying. Alice and I always turned to her expecting, and receiving, a thoughtful, even-tempered response to our problems.

She must have gone literally years without the lift of a new coat, or "good shoes," or even just a nice new dress. Of course Dad's "good suit" when I went away to college was still his wedding suit!

On the surface Dad was by far the dominant and stronger character. His weakness was that his problems got him down. Not literally, however, for when things got particularly difficult he only worked all the harder. But he went into periods of withdrawn melancholy.

I would sometimes be angry about them at the time. But as I look back now and attempt to put myself in those same shoes— utterly impossible as that is to do—I am indeed quite charitable.

Actually, Dad's personality had many facets. One of them was a fierce independence. He would do things himself. He would not be waited upon. Also, he was bound that he "would not lie around and die in that Jefferson hospital." He was done in by leukemia. There were many blood transfusions. I would take him to the hospital and watch and do what I could as fresh new blood dripped into his veins and brought, temporarily, a new flush to his cheeks and renewed strength. I brought him home from the hospital at 3 A.M., following a transfusion, so that he would not have to spend a night in the hospital.

But that could go on only so long. The blood just got too thin. Finally he would have to use both hands to pick up the pitcher to pour milk or iced tea at the table. But he would do that. That was his job. When he could not walk upstairs he would turn around, sit down on the steps and hoist himself up, a step at a time, using both arms and legs. No one was going to carry him around!

He did not have his wish—not quite. He did draw his last breath in the hospital. But he was there only a matter of hours.

Anyone who has read earlier parts of this book will have gained the impression that Dad tended to be a perfectionist, to be demanding, to be a hard worker, and to believe that many of our present problems would be solved if everyone would work, save, and not depend on the government!

Obviously, he had some pretty frustrating times as society as a whole tended to do more and more things for individuals.

184

So many, many things were happening, and changing, *in no time at all.*

*   *   *

And finally—

This is no time, in this piece of prosaic prose, to start quoting great literary figures. But Samuel Johnson, that great English writer who had his share of troubles, once observed, "A man used to vicissitudes is not easily dejected."

Similarly a boy growing up on a farm in the twenties and thirties under the circumstances just reviewed, would not be likely to find anything particularly difficult in subsequent years. It hasn't been. For me it has been pretty much a downhill pull since that time.

I can't avoid reflecting on that fact as I sit on a plane beside some 10-year-old boy as he calmly pops his bubble gum and reads his comic book while the raw power of the jet sends us hurtling through space at 600 miles an hour. This is his world; but he takes it for granted. It is not just that the jet is here but that his parents have money enough to make this such a casual experience for him. Is his whole life going to be blasé? Will there be no exciting new experiences for him? About what will he be writing his grandchildren as he tries to give them some one-generation-to-another perspective? What will he do for fun? Will his life be a downhill pull? But then, I remind myself, with a bit of effort I must admit, that such thinking indicates a hardening of intellectual arteries—a feeling that there's nothing new Out There. That I don't believe; it's just that I can't imagine it.

Probably as changes have come along this feeling on the part of the older generation has always been thus. The difference, if there is a difference, comes in the astonishing rate of change in the last few decades. But that is the point I stressed way back there in the opening paragraphs. So I close, proving that I have come full circle or am beginning to repeat myself!